A CASE FOR KINDNESS

Lisa Barrickman ♡

#KindnessWorks

40 WAYS TO LOVE AND INSPIRE OTHERS

LISA BARRICKMAN

WORTHY®
Inspired

Library of Congress Control Number: 2017938199

ISBN: 978-1-68397-032-3

Printed in the United States of America

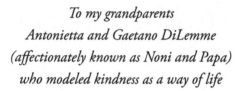

To my grandparents
Antonietta and Gaetano DiLemme
(affectionately known as Noni and Papa)
who modeled kindness as a way of life

CONTENTS

I expect to pass through life but once.
If therefore, there be any kindness
I can show, or any good thing I can do
to any fellow being, let me do it now,
and not defer or neglect it,
as I shall not pass this way again.

—

William Penn

INTRODUCTION

I STOOD IN FRONT of the milestone birthday cards and wondered if I should just buy them in bulk. One at a time, month after month, friends were celebrating their big 4-0 birthdays.

With each celebration, and every fortieth birthday Facebook post, I started to feel the impending arrival of my day, my turn to welcome number forty. Was it really a big deal? After some deliberation, I decided on yes. Yes, it was a big deal.

In my experience, turning forty felt liberating. Up to that point, I had been creating the framework for adulthood. I was always planning for the next thing: school, career, marriage, house, kids. Each step brought me closer to answering the classic question, "What are you going to be when you grow up?" Well, now I was up. All of the pieces were in place and ready to enjoy. There would certainly be bumps, changes, and unexpected turns along the way, but I had acquired some wisdom in forty years to handle it. Another reason to throw confetti.

It became clear that my fortieth birthday was worth celebrating, but I wasn't quite sure how to do it. A family vacation? A just-me-and-my-husband getaway? A girls' weekend? A party?

Nothing was jumping out at me.

As I prayed about this rite of passage, a flood of gratitude overpowered any prospective birthday wish. I glanced back at forty imperfect yet beautifully blessed years, and I was thankful for all of it. Thankful for life.

I wanted my celebration to reflect this spirit of gratitude.

My initial intention was a family mission trip for Spring Break. I looked into options around the country, but my youngest child was only six years old at the time and I couldn't find a good fit.

After some thought, I had an *aha* moment one morning in the shower (my own personal think box). Somewhere between lather and rinse, I decided to do an act of kindness every day for forty days leading up to my birthday. We didn't need to travel to a far off place to help others, we could scatter love right in the midst our daily routines. That decision began an incredible journey: Forty Days of Kindness.

Before beginning my Forty Days of Kindness project, I had some cards made that shared the words of William Penn:

I expect to pass through life but once. If therefore, there be any kindness I can show or any good thing I can do to any fellow being, let me do it now and not defer or neglect it, as I shall not pass this way again.

The back of the cards simply said, "Kindness is contagious . . . pass it on." A stack of these kindness cards, a daily journal, a list of realistic ideas, and an open heart to receive God's guidance each day was all it took to begin spreading kindness!

The number forty, mentioned one hundred forty-six times in the Bible, is believed to be the amount of time necessary to complete a work (think forty weeks of pregnancy). Something remarkable happened to me and my family in forty days. While any act of kindness is a blessing, practicing kindness for forty *consecutive* days created a habit of seeking ways to help others. I began to see my day's purpose and the people around me differently. I slowed down, looked more closely, and thought more intently about how to make a difference in someone else's life every day. I was continually reminded that we are all connected—we're all in this together. Every child of God has the capacity, in ordinary moments, to change a heart in an extraordinary way.

To my surprise, the best part of the journey has been the ripple effect it brought with it. My kids began asking, as soon as they got home from school, about my act of kindness for the day. Bursting with great ideas for spreading kindness, they were excited to share their own acts of kindness and the moments they'd witnessed others acting out of love. We could not stop after forty days. We had been transformed.

My family's kindness journey was something we had kept very quiet; we hadn't even shared it with our closest friends and family members. We didn't want any part of it to be about recognition. But as time passed and the impact stuck with us, I couldn't shake the thought that the experience was too good not to share. We had discovered a simple treasure, capable of creating happiness, focus, and connection. So we shared it with our pastors, Pastor Krewson and Pastor Cindy. They were instantly enthusiastic, and our church implemented the plan. As I beheld the infectious nature of kindness flourish within a community, I was sincerely thankful for having shared my story.

Forty Days of Kindness culminated on our church's "Rally Sunday," which kicks off the new Sunday school year. Over one hundred people participated, translating to four thousand acts of kindness!

Implementing the project was a breeze—it was a great first act of kindness for a small team of people who took the lead. We advertised for a few weeks in advance, sharing the essence of the program and the dates. We created a bulletin board featuring inspirational quotes about kindness and a sign up sheet. We included a resource table next to the bulletin board where participants could take a stack of ten kindness cards and a list of ideas for acts of kindness. And we offered opportunities to share the experience with others. During the forty days, our pastors would occasionally share the stories they were receiving from participants, stories of Christ's love on the move through our simple acts of love.

Forty days of kindness was such a success we did it again the next year, adding a community service day for the fortieth day of kindness. We reached over ten local agencies in one day. "Community Service Saturday" has continued to grow and enrich the lives of those giving and receiving.

And the ripples didn't end there. A woman from our church led her grandchildren in a kindness project to celebrate her seventieth birthday. (They even made her a collage highlighting the kindness scattered in her honor!) A friend of hers heard what they were doing and initiated the project at her church in New Jersey, and they are on round two of Forty Days of Kindness. My mother-in-law loved the idea and took it to her church in Ohio. Then her brother and sister-in-law led the initiative with their church in Florida for the forty days of Lent. Ripple. Ripple. Ripple.

Even with only a few people leading kindness initiatives, over twenty thousand acts of kindness were sprinkled around the country. Imagine the ripples we can all make together! I invite you to join in and spread some kindness wherever you are. Throughout the pages of this book, you will find real-life stories and valuable resources for showing kindness. You may even want to launch Forty Days of Kindness with your family, scout troop, sports team, school, workplace, church community, or neighborhood. What a profound way to unite a group through a common experience, all while making a difference within your own heart and your community.

I'm excited for you to begin your kindness adventure! As we journey together through forty ways to love and inspire others, my prayer is that each chapter will fill you with God's love and equip you to be His hands in the everyday moments of life.

CHAPTER 1

THE RIPPLE EFFECT

HAVE YOU EVER BEEN SO MOVED by another person's actions that you started to see the world in a new light? Brighter. Brimming with goodness. So much goodness that you just wanted to keep it going. And going.

Many years ago, a person whose name I don't recall and whose face I wouldn't recognize left a lasting impact on my life with the simple gift of kindness. Kindness . . . the decision to reach out to another human being with love, just because it's a good way to live.

It happened when I sat down on an airplane—I didn't know that the gentleman seated next to me would turn out to be an angel in disguise. And he didn't know that the adorable infant in my arms could wake the dead with his colicky cry . . . nor did he know that I suffer from severe motion sickness. If everything had gone as planned, he would have gotten through the entire flight without having to learn either of those interesting tidbits. But that is not how it played out. Not even close.

A quick one-hour flight became a nightmare when winter weather quite literally took us all by storm. With endless delays and ferocious turbulence, one hour turned into five, a sleeping baby turned into a screeching siren, and I turned green. In the midst of it all, the stranger beside me leaned over and calmly said, "Is there anything I can do to help you?" And help he did. Even after I desperately handed him my disgruntled travel buddy so I could vomit, he continued to selflessly offer his help. And he stayed beside me all the way to the finish line, complete with a gateless exit from the aircraft right into the roaring blizzard!

Safe and sound, with a jubilant sigh of relief, I expressed my overabundance of gratitude. I knew I would never see this person again, and I also knew I would never forget his comforting kindness. He had given me so many valuable gifts that day, without any monetary cost—acceptance, time, patience, a glass of water, an extra hand. His example was a powerful reminder that we all have the ability, in everyday life and in exceptional moments, to be the hands and feet of God on earth.

The warm memories of that chilling day have never faded, because my eyes were forever opened to the power of kindness. The ripple created by a compassionate stranger continues a decade later, inspiring my celebration of kindness and now flowing into yours. When we set kindness into motion, it takes on a life of its own. It extends far beyond our sight, beyond our comprehension.

During Forty Days of Kindness at church, one friend eagerly embraced the kindness project, while her husband, Lloyd, was not interested. At all. His exact words were an emphatic, "I'm not doing it."

About a week into the forty days, he came home from a grocery run and shared that he had gathered up the carts in the parking lot and put them where they belong. Astonishingly, he proceeded to say that this was his act of kindness for the day. He admitted that kindness had been on his mind since everyone else seemed so into it, and he thought he would give it a try. (Ripple!) To this day, he still gathers up the carts whenever there is a need.

While at the store one day, Lloyd surprised even himself with a gesture that involved spending more time in line. He only had a few items to purchase, while the woman behind him had a cart filled to the top with groceries. Her fussy toddler had clearly had enough of the afternoon errand, so Lloyd invited the frazzled mom to go in front of him. Her gratitude and relieved smile further encouraged him in his kindness efforts, and he continued sending ripples of goodness out into the world.

As we dive into the splendor of kindness, we are creating endless possibilities with each gesture of love we release. Amelia Earhart describes it this way, "A single act of kindness throws out roots in all directions and the roots spring up and make new trees."

We are all standing on the shore with shimmering pebbles in our hands. Let's cast them into the water and marvel at the ripples!

Whoever believes in me, as Scripture has said,
rivers of living water will flow from within them.
JOHN 7:38 NIV

CHAPTER 2

CELEBRATION OF APPRECIATION

THE DIRECTOR OF THE CHURCH worship team, Daniel, approached the Forty Days of Kindness sign-up table with tears teetering from the pools in his eyes. He was certain God had led him to church that morning to hear the presentation on the upcoming kindness initiative.

Daniel had recently gotten the news that his favorite middle school teacher was in poor health and in a nursing home. On the way to church that morning, he was thinking about the profound impact this dedicated mentor had made on his life. With a gleaming saxophone in his hand, Daniel credited his exceptional teacher for bringing out his love of music and leading him to a career as a college music professor. A reminder about simple acts of kindness was just the push he needed to reach out to his teacher with a gesture of sincere gratitude.

Daniel thought about his own students, and realized that his teacher had indirectly marked their lives too. He was eager to get to work on a thank-you note; his words were sure to be a genuine gift, bringing joy to the reader and peace to the writer.

If you have ever received a letter like this, you know it is a piece of mail that will escape the trashcan and be tucked in a safe place. It's a cherished treasure, a tangible reminder that our work and our lives have made a difference, and a word of encouragement for a tough day.

Maybe you're thinking of someone who has made a difference in your life. Why not grab a notecard and let them know? The mere sight of "real mail" and a handwritten note is enough to make someone's day.

As you get into a groove of spreading kindness, you will quickly discover unlimited opportunities to express appreciation. One of my most memorable acts of kindness involved creatively thanking someone who selflessly serves the community.

My kids and I were picking up the dry cleaning. As the parade of clothes spun past on the conveyer, I couldn't help but notice some work uniforms. I asked if there was an order for someone in public service that we could treat, and the pleasant woman behind the counter started to beam. She told me that a fantastic police officer named Pete would be in the next day. He always went above and beyond the call of duty. And he always picked up his uniform on the same day. We added his payment to our order and left a kindness card for him to receive instead of his bill. The woman working was so moved by the act of kindness that she asked if she could have a couple of the cards. Ripple.

There are countless people in our midst who serve to keep our day-to-day lives running smoothly. A simple gesture to thank them can go a long way. A note and some cookies left in the mailbox for the mailman (Girl Scout Thanks-a-Lots are great for this). A hot chocolate delivery to road workers on a cold day or lemonade on a hot day. Flowers brought to the front office at church or our children's school. Coffee for the bus driver. A handshake and warm words of thanks to a military officer. A note of appreciation taped to the trashcan for the trash collector to find. Lunch delivery for a favorite hair stylist. An evening snack dropped off at the local fire station. And with each action, a silent prayer for the person we are reaching out to.

If you really want to get creative, here are a few fun ways to say "you're sweet" with sweets. Just attach a notecard to the treat and brighten someone's day:

Milky Way: Thanks! You are out of this world.

Extra gum: Thanks for going the Extra mile.

Fortune Cookies: It's my good fortune to know you.

Snickers: Thanks for the laughs and the Snickers.

Hershey's Hugs and Kisses: Hugs and Kisses for a job well done.

Nutella: I can *Nutella* how much I appreciate you.

M&Ms: Many Many Thanks!

Andes Mints: Thanks for your commit-*mint*.

Thanks for your encourage-*mint*.

Swedish Fish: You are o-*Fish*-ally the greatest.

LifeSavers: Thanks for being such a Lifesaver.
Take 5: Thanks for your hard work. Take 5!

Whether we are thanking someone for changing our lives, making us smile, or serving us throughout a typical day, being appreciated is appreciated! Through every word of thanks, every act of gratitude, every whispered prayer, we're encouraging others and showing them that their lives are meaningful. We're letting them know they haven't gone unnoticed. We're changing the way we view the people in motion all around us and inspiring them to do the same. We're making the world smaller. Brighter. We're creating a change in the atmosphere . . . a celebration of appreciation.

Every time I think of you, I thank my God.
And whenever I mention you in my prayers, it makes me happy.
PHILIPPIANS 1:3–4 CEV

CHAPTER 3

EYES WIDE OPEN

"MOM," MY SON JACK WHISPERED as he urgently tapped me and pointed at the ground. The child sitting in front of us at the soccer stadium was gaping at a perfectly sprinkled ice-cream cone through tear-filled eyes. Poor kid hadn't even enjoyed one lick when his treat bit the dust!

The distraught boy's father was alone at the game with three young kids, so it would have been a tall order for him to leave his seat to rectify the ice cream casualty. Before I could say a word, Jack asked if he could run out to the concession stand and get another cone.

With his Philadelphia Union Soccer scarf around his neck and a radiant sprinkled cone in his hand, he jogged up the concrete steps back to our seats. I watched my "little boy" make the day of another little boy, and I honestly don't know which kid had the bigger smile when the ice cream exchanged hands.

This was many months after my forty-day kindness project concluded, and I was still in awe of the lasting impact it had on my family. It was no longer about planning something or wondering what our act of kindness would be each day. It now simply meant that our eyes were open to what was happening around us, and our hearts were open to making the situation better, whatever that entailed.

During this time of transformation, my husband came home from a business trip to New York with an incredible story. I remember him walking in the house and simply saying, "Something happened today."

Where he typically would have been looking at his phone or reading on the subway, he, too, had been changed by our commitment to kindness. His new state of mind had him looking around, eyes wide open. As the train came to a stop, he noticed that an elderly gentleman had stood up too soon. The fitful jerking of the subway jostled him, and it was clear that the man was losing his balance and heading toward the floor. Fast.

My husband sprinted to the front of the train and caught the man in his arms. It was a little awkward at first for him to be holding a stranger on a Manhattan subway, but both men were filled with gratitude. One for what he had avoided, the other for what he had gained.

As we all became more in touch with our surroundings—spending more time looking up at the world around us—we were astounded by the endless needs we could meet for others throughout the course of a day. Some big. Some small. All meaningful. All doable.

We can help the person struggling to get the baby stroller through the door. Pop a few quarters into a parking meter when the time is expired. Give a tissue, a pen, an umbrella. Ask someone who looks lost if they need directions. Offer our spot in line to the person in a big rush. Go out of our way to bring an animal to safety. Alert the management that a car in the parking lot has its lights on. By being attentive, we'll know exactly what to do.

An exciting bonus of responding to the needs around us is the effect of these acts of kindness on those who witness them. I like to think that these people get "splashed" by kindness. They aren't pouring out the kindness, and they aren't directly drenched by it. But they are there. And they get splashed! Chances are, someone saw that cute guy in the suit racing down the subway aisle to catch a falling stranger. They may have even gone home that night and shared the story. Maybe they were more willing to step in to help someone else because of the splashing.

Usually when we see an act of kindness, it has a way of staying with us. Many years ago, on an ugly rainy day, I noticed a car parked near me with a black garbage bag covering one of the windows. There was a note attached to the bag that said: "Sorry for messing with your car, but it was pouring and your window was down. I thought this might help." It was signed, "Concerned stranger." Unforgettable.

Just seeing love around us is uplifting. Restorative. It gives us that warm, goose-bumpy feeling, reminding us that pure goodness is still alive and well.

So when we are out reacting to the world with kindness, we can be encouraged that our love has a three-way impact. It pleases the pourer, delights the drenched, and stirs up the splashed. With open eyes, we can see kindness reaching far and wide.

Staying alert leads to the great privilege of helping another person at the perfect time. Here we all are. Together. The more we reach out in unity, the more unified we will be.

———————————

So now I am giving you a new commandment:
Love each other. Just as I have loved you,
you should love each other.

JOHN 13:34

CHAPTER 4

COURAGEOUS KINDNESS

"I DIDN'T GIVE IT ANY THOUGHT. I just knew. I knew I needed to walk over to her." Compelled to approach the crying twenty-something woman at the airport ticket counter, my mother-in-law described her conviction as the work of the Holy Spirit. No contemplation necessary. Only action.

The distraught traveler needed to get to Chicago in a hurry, and an unexpected issue with her credit card couldn't be rectified for twenty-four hours. Her parents were already in the air, also heading to the Windy City, so they were unaware of this complication and unable to help. Bottom line, this girl needed a ticket. And fast.

Without hesitation, my mother-in-law took a leap of faith.

She shared that she couldn't afford to give the ticket as a gift, but she would happily pay for it and share her contact information to be paid back later. Overwhelmed with gratitude, tears streaming, the young woman accepted this joyous delivery of goodness.

A marveling airport employee, splashed by this act of kindness, declared, "We just met an angel."

The following week, a letter arrived from the young woman and her father. Teeming with appreciation, it included a check for the ticket, and a request for a favorite charity they could support to keep the generosity going. The letter even showed further impact of the good deed, as the dad shared: "My wife and I have told this story to quite a few people over the past few days, and everyone is amazed and touched. This will become part of our family lore."

Through heartfelt words, he went on to reveal that his daughter was rushing to Chicago on that desperate day to attend her grandmother's funeral; without the compassion of a stranger, she would have missed it. And they would have missed her, making the day even more trying.

Powerful.

Inspired.

Kindness.

Sometimes we are called to step out in faith, to take a risk as we help someone, even when we don't understand the purpose. The best part about trusting and following God's lead is the unfolding story. When we have the privilege of seeing the full picture, seeing what He had in mind all along, it is nothing short of miraculous.

But what if we are never invited into the whole story? What if the details are never filled in, like a book sporadically missing chapters? Just as easily, the girl and her family could have chosen not to contact my mother-in-law. The reason for the tears could have remained a mystery, the money lost. What then?

Then, we look more closely at the phrase *a leap of faith*, and we put our focus on the word *faith*. In the words of Martin Luther King Jr., "Faith is taking the first step, even when you don't see the whole staircase." When God nudges us, we can trust that we are needed, even if it involves risk. We may not be able to see why or what happened next, but God certainly does. Ultimately, we are called to do our part and leave the rest to Him.

The greatest impact from a good deed may be contrary to what is obvious. In my mother-in-law's compassionate airport inter-action, the greatest impact made could have been the effect on an observer of the moment who desperately needed a message of hope in humanity. Even if the money had been lost, even if the extreme appreciation from the family was missing, there still would have been incredible gain. Many lives are touched by our actions, regardless of the visible outcome.

Kindness takes courage. It isn't easy to be vulnerable for the sake of others, or for the sake of our faith, but a "bring it on" attitude can change lives . . . maybe even our own! When God takes us by the hand and leads us out of our safe house, He's got plans. Big, beautiful plans. And we get to be the angels.

We can stand up for the outsider even when we risk being judged. Invite the uninvited. Forgive. We can be still with a friend in the darkness, embracing their pain rather than looking away. Put ourselves way out there to help. Perhaps make a wholehearted effort to connect with someone we don't exactly enjoy . . . and find ourselves pleasantly surprised. We could defend the name of a person often misunderstood or risk looking different to support a loved one. Share time or money when it's in short supply, trusting it will come back to us. We can celebrate the heroes and public servants in our community—for some, courageous kindness is a way of life.

Developing kindness is often compared to training a muscle; the more we exercise this virtue, the stronger it will become. As acts of love seep into our day-to-day lives, we will be increasingly willing to take leaps of faith. We'll find the walls of our comfort zone stretching as we faithfully serve with the hands of Jesus. And our actions will leave a lasting impact.

We all need a fierce reminder that love really is winning; it's a profound experience that sets the record straight. With courage, we can provide a message of hope through our actions.

This was perfectly expressed in the thank-you letter to the airport angel: "Truly good people still exist in the world. I will never forget your kindness."

This is my command—be strong and courageous!
Do not be afraid or discouraged.
For the LORD your God is with you wherever you go.

JOSHUA 1:9

CHAPTER 5

DELIGHTFUL DRIVER

ENORMOUS SNOWBANKS overwhelmed the neighborhoods; tracks running down each glistening pile squealed of childhood sledding fun. But steering a car between those massive mounds wasn't quite as exhilarating.

I turned down a narrow side road and could not believe my eyes—an ambitious fellow driver was attempting to turn around in the middle of the road. Now, remember: the sides of the street were blocked by slick white mountains! Drive. Reverse. Slight turn. Drive. Reverse. Slight turn. And so it went for a full country song on my radio. With no way out, I wasn't sure what was taking more abuse, the car's gearshift or my patience!

About halfway through this winter driving display (and halfway through my forty-day kindness project), I realized I did not have a plan for my good deed that day. So I decided to seize the moment and actively exercise patience. Rather than gripping the wheel, fogging up the windows with smoke from my ears, and complaining aloud to myself about this ridiculous time-suck, I did something else. I took a deep breath, waved, and smiled. I gave the gifts of understanding and courtesy, and before I knew it, I was back in motion.

My annoyance would not have changed the situation, and frankly, the waiting became much more tolerable once I was in a calm state. I'm sure it also made a huge difference for the other driver. Imagine how much worse it would have been if I had started honking or throwing snowballs!

Keeping an attitude of kindness can help us as much as it does the people around us; it colors everything with hues of positivity. Our actions. Our feelings. Our outlook. Just like the glow of a brilliant sunset brings warmth and color to everything around it, so the color of kindness tints whatever it touches. Kindness can turn gray into cheerful yellow. It brings out a smile instead of a scowl.

For those who drive, I think we can safely say that we all see opportunities for positivity on the road. And we also must admit we have moments behind the wheel that don't go so well—moments when assistance or forgiveness are worth their weight in premium gasoline. We can offer genuine consideration to others, showing love and keeping our own blood pressure down in the process.

As we're cruising through our days, let's strive for "delightful driver," rather than "road rage." We can give up that rock-star parking spot. Let someone merge even if we think they are in the wrong. Honk less, smile more. Think about what we appreciate from other drivers on the road and do that! Give the benefit of the doubt. We can take responsibility for our own driving mess-ups. Go out of our way to let someone make a tricky left turn. Express thanks to a helpful driver. If it's uncomfortable to stop to help, we can call 9-1-1 to report an accident or broken-down vehicle. And lastly (a message I desperately need), we can slow down and give ourselves plenty of time to get to the next place. We are more likely to be patient when we aren't in a rush.

Ironically, the very next day after the snowbank turn-around incident, I found myself on the receiving end of kindness via de-lightful driving. We were sitting at a red light when a man in the truck beside us rolled down his window and gently tapped his horn to get my attention. He thoughtfully let me know that one of my brake lights had burned out. Our thirty-second exchange was extremely helpful, since I spend little time behind my car while it's traveling down the road!

This experience was a great reminder of other useful observations we can make on behalf of our fellow drivers: Let someone know that a tire looks low, the trunk is unlatched, something is hanging out the door, or the gas tank is open.

As a bonus, my kids were in the car during the much-appreciated gesture of kindness from the man in the truck. Since we were right in the middle of our kindness mission, they were excited to be on the other end of the equation. We talked about other times we'd received kindness, and tapping into those pleasant feelings fueled our efforts even more. Also, seeing the effect of such a quick, easy act of kindness brought us back to the sentiment that we can make an extraordinary difference in ordinary moments.

Taking kindness on the road fits right into our day-to-day travels. No detour necessary. Just a tankful of love.

Always be humble and gentle. Be patient with each other, making allowance for each other's faults because of your love.
EPHESIANS 4:2

CHAPTER 6

KIDS
FOR KINDNESS

AFTER FINISHING AN IMPRESSIVE six-minute mile, a sixth-grade boy notices a classmate struggling to finish his final laps. Without hesitation, he runs out on the track to offer encouragement, trotting beside the other boy the rest of the way. Kindness.

A little girl drops her pencil case during class, and the contents spill out everywhere. Having just learned about the power of helping others, the rest of the kids in the room dive to the ground to assist their friend. Instant cleanup. Huge smiles. Kindness.

A toddler skins his knee at a park. He sits on the ground in a puddle of tears. A concerned child runs over to offer a hug and a juice box. Kindness.

A teenager spots a new student eating alone in the cafeteria.

She walks over and asks simply, "Would you like to eat with us?" Three years later . . . their friendship continues. Kindness.

Every Friday, kindness brightens the halls of an elementary school, thanks to the loving hands of one group of second graders. The entire class joyfully spends twenty minutes volunteering throughout the school. (One of the kids even wears a festive shirt that says "Kind people are my kind of people!") Each student finds a special way to intentionally make others' lives better through small acts of kindness. They sharpen pencils. Organize library books. Put away gym equipment. Help the custodian. Deliver mail. Kindness.

True stories. Real impact.

There is a beautiful spirit of sincerity encircling each kindness initiated by children. Their actions are typically without financial cost and straight from the heart, with powerful effects.

Particularly when kids show kindness toward other kids, the impact can be life changing. Being a child, tween, or teen is hard work. They're navigating new stages of life. Figuring out where they fit. Seeking acceptance and fearing rejection. Not always feeling heard or seen.

Kids find and bring great comfort when they have each other's backs. When they reach out, like the boy helping his classmate finish the race. When they stand up for someone being mistreated or excluded. When they are the first to offer forgiveness and acceptance. Unfortunately, these gestures aren't always easy; they can come with great social cost. Being kind isn't always associated with being "cool."

And while it's inevitable that showing kindness will sometimes be difficult, embracing its importance can make the price feel much less significant. By instilling this divine virtue in our own children and the children we work with, we equip them to make a dramatic difference in the lives of other kids . . . and in the world!

As we seek to create an altruistic mindset in kids, one of the most valuable gifts we can give them is the opportunity to show love to others. Once they experience the joy of giving, they will begin to independently recognize ways to sprinkle kindness, even at a very young age. I recently watched a kindergartener hold the door for an entire car line of students. He just stood there smiling, until all the kids were inside the building.

Dr. Patty O'Grady, an expert in positive psychology, says that "kindness changes the brain by the experience of kindness. Children and adolescents do not learn kindness by only thinking about it and talking about it. Kindness is best learned by feeling it, so they can reproduce it."

And while the image of kids multiplying kindness is exciting enough on its own, there are also incredible benefits for them as the givers. Spreading kindness increases happiness, gratitude, health, and self-esteem, while decreasing bullying, depression, anxiety, and stress.

So where do we start?

Chances are, the children in our lives already have great ideas for showing love to others. Begin by asking them for their thoughts. Then spark more ideas by sharing kid-friendly and kid-inspired good deeds.

They can donate old toys and books to charity. Create a video greeting for a long-distance friend or family member. Write positive messages in sidewalk chalk on the playground. Start a kindness club at school. Notice the children standing alone at recess or at the park and ask them to play. Decorate pillowcases and take them to a children's hospital. Bring an extra snack to school for a classmate. Have a lemonade stand and donate the proceeds to Alex's Lemonade Stand (alexslemonade.org) to support childhood cancer research. Support a favorite charity—request donations instead of birthday gifts. Bake delicious treats to share with others. Make placemats using original artwork covered in clear contact paper; take them to a soup kitchen or homeless shelter. Check out ColoraSmile.org—coloring pages can be printed out and mailed in, then they are distributed to military troops, nursing homes, and others in need of a smile!

In my experience working with kids, I have consistently seen their excitement to serve. Often, they simply need a plan and gentle guidance. By providing opportunities and planting seeds of kindness in kids, we prepare the next generation for success. We are igniting a light inside them that will shine throughout their lives.

Who knows, if more kids learn to prioritize good works, *kind* could become the new *cool!*

Don't let anyone think less of you because you are young.
Be an example to all believers in what you say, in the way you live,
in your love, your faith, and your purity.

1 TIMOTHY 4:12

CHAPTER 7

RAIN OR SHINE

CHANCE OF MORNING RAIN: 80 percent. Opportunity for showing kindness: 100 percent.

I was ready. The front seat of my car held a new, navy-blue umbrella with a kindness card tucked in the carrying case. When the rain showed up, I would give the umbrella to someone stuck in the showers or leave it at a bus stop.

Simple enough.

The dark sky opened and it was go time . . . time to find a rain-rescue-recipient! As I drove around, I became unintentionally selective; I was looking for the "right" person. My eyes combed the streets for someone who *really* needed a break. Someone who would benefit from a shiny new umbrella beyond one drizzly day.

I eventually came to my senses and recognized that anyone standing in the rain could use shelter. Period. And I started to fall even more in love with the beauty of kindness. Kindness has the capacity to transcend typical boundaries like age, faith, politics, gender, language, ethnicity, and wealth. When it comes to spreading and receiving love, we can all stand as one.

I had gotten myself so hung up on finding someone truly "deserving" of my good deed that I'd lost sight of the truth—we all deserve kindness. Titus 3:4–5 says, "But when God our Savior revealed his kindness and love, he saved us, not because of the righteous things we had done, but because of his mercy." God showers us with His kindness. It is a gift each one of us can receive. A gift that we can in turn share with one another.

And by the time I figured this out, it stopped raining!

I had missed my chance.

The sun peeked through the clouds, and new light illuminated my kindness mission. Later, when I was writing in my journal, I shared a quote from Johann Wolfgang von Goethe. He said, "Kindness is the golden chain by which society is bound together." More than two hundred years have passed since he expressed that thought, but the relevance of his message remains. In our constantly changing world, we can always count on the persistent, pervasive impact of helping others. Kindness has some serious staying power!

As we seek ways to become a link on that golden chain of kindness, we can find practical, weather-related opportunities throughout the year. Just as the rain will happily soak any one of us, we are all subject to the challenges Mother Nature presents.

With a handful of supplies, we'll be equipped to scatter good-ness—rain or shine. We can take a thermos of hot chocolate and to-go cups to a chilly sporting event. Gather up the family and rake a friend's leaves. Shovel a neighbor's driveway . . . just because. Organize a winter car wash when the road salt is making a mess . . . then donate the proceeds to a favorite charity. Supply a cooler of popsicles on a sizzling day. Leave a bottle of sunscreen at a park with a kindness card attached to it. Visit redcross.org to make an online donation or volunteer for disaster-relief efforts including hurricanes, tornadoes, wildfires, floods, earthquakes, and super-storms. Stock the car with gel hand warmers to share on a super cold day. They'd go great with that extra umbrella.

Speaking of an umbrella . . . you might be wondering what happened to the one I wasn't able to give away. It turned out to be an incredible blessing! An awesome "God-wink" moment.

The umbrella was still hanging out on the floor of my minivan a couple of weeks after my missed kindness opportunity. It was buried under sweatshirts, a backpack, a bag of goldfish crackers, and a pair of boots I'd been meaning to return. But it was there.

I was driving through my neighborhood when the sky sud-denly turned gravel-gray, and I could hear the thunder marching in. As I neared my turn, I noticed two people I frequently saw walking together: an elderly gentleman and his caregiver. Slowly and watchfully, arm in arm, they were making their way home. But they were still about a football field away. And the rain didn't seem interested in waiting.

I didn't know them, but I rolled down my window, reaching out with love and a navy-blue umbrella. The surprised caregiver gratefully accepted the shelter and quickly opened it to shield the light, steady drops of rain.

As I turned the corner toward home, a blustering curtain of water descended from above. And I was relieved that the two men were covered. Protected.

I could barely see the road in front of me, but I *could* see, sharp and clear, the hand of God in that moment. And I saw the connection we share with *everyone*. The enormity in our small acts of love.

Today's forecast predicts hope and happiness. Kindness is expected to spread throughout the region!

There will be a shelter to give shade from the heat by day, and refuge and protection from the storm and the rain.
Isaiah 4:6 nasb

CHAPTER 8

ALL IN THE FAMILY

THE DINNER TABLE was festively decorated, complete with a ceramic cupcake centerpiece and three beautifully embellished, construction-paper birthday cards. Dinner from my favorite Mexican restaurant was in Styrofoam, which meant I didn't have to cook or clean up. *Score.* I looked around at my little family, thinking the day couldn't get any better. Then, curiously, my husband Josh stood up from the table and walked into the garage.

He came back inside with a cake in his arms. *What!* It wasn't just any old cake. It was my forever favorite—chocolate sponge cake bottom, chocolate chip ice cream center, buttercream frosting. I hadn't had it in years because the ice cream shop by our house had closed, which was a heartbreaking loss. Birthdays had not been the same without my favorite cake.

My husband knew this gesture would make my day, so he

did his research and discovered that the delicacy was now available twenty minutes from his office. He ordered the cake the day before, left work on his lunch break to pick it up, and stored it in a freezer at work for the rest of the day. The sweetest surprise.

I'm sure I also opened an actual birthday present that year, purchased from a store and placed in a festive bag without tissue paper. Any specific memory of the gift is lost, yet I haven't forgotten my husband's effort in making my day extra special. His thoughtfulness was the perfect ending to a day filled with simple, loving actions. The icing on the cake!

When we think about acts of kindness, we often associate the phrase with doing nice things for strangers. And while random acts of kindness can absolutely be fantastic, opportunities for spreading intentional, planned, on-purpose kindness are right under our roof.

We can fill up the tank when we use a family member's or roommate's car. Take someone's chore for the day. Deliver breakfast in bed. Include a sibling when friends are over. Create compliment jars for each person in the house. Organize an impromptu date night. Give the gift of uninterrupted time. Listen intently. Fix something. Surprise the children with a day off school for a family activity. (Kids—you're welcome!) Put an encouraging note in a sports bag, a lunch box, or an instrument case. Fill a vase with flowers. Let someone else pick the movie. Make dinner or clean up when it isn't expected. Plan a family game night and pull out the dreaded game that someone else loves. Plan a surprise visit to a friend. Show up with coffee. It all comes down to being attentive and giving the priceless gift of our time.

One wintry day during my forty-day kindness adventure, I happened to have Josh's car because he was doing some work on mine. Now, if you live in a place without the fluffy white stuff you may not understand, but trust me, it's not all pretty. The black exterior of Josh's car appeared to be a crackling white, like every other car on the road. Winter rock salt paints itself on everything and makes a total mess. So there is always that one sunny day after a storm when the car wash is the most happening place in town.

For my act of kindness that day, I simply sat in the ridiculous car wash line to get his ride nice and sparkly. I can't be sure that I would have done this without my commitment to kindness. I might have considered it and then kept on driving when I saw the line wrapped around the building. Committing to kindness pushes us from intention to action, especially when it comes to the people closest to us. It's easy to lose the sense of urgency to go wild with kindness toward the people we love the most.

How often do we take for granted the people with a front-row seat to our lives? The people who witness our best and worst moments—fighting for the bathroom, enduring those first morning breaths before we've gotten to the toothbrush. Of all the people in the world, God blessed us with an intimate team to do life with . . . side by side. Rather than rushing past each other, let's actively commit to our closest people.

We can commit to fiercely loving these special people with our actions, but also with our attitudes. I am admittedly quick to be a bear with my family, in a way I wouldn't dream of doing when I walk out the door. Can you relate? So often we can be on our best behavior with others, but we save our absolute worst for those we love most. In my own life, I see a dramatic change in the overall atmosphere of my home when I focus on being my best self, even within my most comfortable environment. Just because our families will keep on loving us when we act ugly, doesn't make it a good idea.

When we remember who deserves our very best, we can make an enormous difference for ourselves and for the loves of our lives. Even with inevitable imperfection, our homes will feel warmer. Sunnier. Let's intentionally serve our families the beautiful, steaming feast . . . not the leftovers.

We can create a great work of love right where we are. The seeds of encouragement and goodness that we plant in our very own gardens can grow into a legacy of kindness that will extend far beyond our lives.

But as for me and my household, we will serve the LORD.
JOSHUA 24:15 NIV

CHAPTER 9

SPIRIT OF KINDNESS

I RAN INTO A CONVENIENCE SHOP for an afternoon coffee splurge and a quick break from writing. Immediately, a young man caught my attention as he went out of his way to grab the door for a mom with a stroller. I was drawn to the gold cross around his neck and his infectious spirit. Sunshine seemed to follow him around the store. He gave a high five to a little boy wearing a superman cape. He complimented a man in a dapper purple shirt. He quickly reached in his pocket when a woman in line came up short. He held the door for a few people as he left. He smiled. Everyone around him smiled.

This.

This, I thought, *is a case for kindness.* With every action, the joyful man was making his case, whether he realized it or not. He wasn't doing anything over the top. He was simply being kind to others on purpose.

The Bible has a fancy title for these Christlike virtues we carry with us through life. The apostle Paul identified nine attributes in his letter to the Galatians, referred to as the fruit of the Spirit: "But when the Holy Spirit controls our lives he will produce this kind of fruit in us: love, joy, peace, patience, kindness, goodness, faithfulness, gentleness, and self-control." (Galatians 5:22–23 TLB).

Jesus left behind His Spirit. Alive within each one of us, it is a pervading gift of empowerment and guidance. Receiving this gift, connecting with Jesus, following His lead, and imitating His character results in a great harvest of abundance. Have you ever contemplated the magnitude of this truth, the promises of the Holy Spirit? The enormity settled on me one day as I listened to the lyrics of Jeremy Camp and Jason Ingram's song, *Same Power*; they remind us of the tremendous power we all possess, "The same power that rose Jesus from the grave."

The Holy Spirit is our power source, providing all that we need for doing life. And Spirit-led living results in Spirit-led giving. Filled with the fruit of the Spirit, we will innately treat others with Christlike qualities, scattering seeds all along our path.

Within the backdrop of an ordinary day, these life-giving virtues show up in our most routine responses to the world around us. They enable us to "be nice," to share a spirit of kindness, and to show big love in small moments.

We can pick up trash that isn't ours. Help the person struggling to reach or carry something. Say "take your time," when someone is rattled. Make eye contact. Tie a little friend's shoe. Take a deep breath and be patient. Offer our seat. Take the shopping cart back to the corral or grab the one that's about to hit someone's car. Give sincere compliments. Be polite. Share an encouraging word. We can let the person with two items jump in front of us in line. Accept responsibility when we mess up. Keep our promises. Post a friendly comment on social media. Be honest. Provide clarity when someone looks confused. Play with the kids. Hug. Make someone laugh. Follow the Golden Rule.

Within such basic suggestions and nestled among our daily comings and goings, the wholesome qualities from Christ's Spirit within us are put into play. Being attentive to these characteristics amplifies the active presence of the Holy Spirit in our hearts and in our harvest.

There's a valuable exercise that can help us recognize the fruit of the Spirit in any given day. Make a list of the nine virtues that make up the fruit of the Spirit. Then go back through just one day, filling in the blanks on how we experienced Christ's virtues and released them into the world. I'm going to give this a try with my last twenty-four hours. Here goes:

Love: Made time in a busy day to have a date with one of my kids.

Joy: Received a package from my sweet friend Ticey. Shared with her that she made my day.

Peace: Listening to piano hymns as I write this, and my heart is full.

Patience: Remained calm and friendly when our dinner

order was forgotten and we had to wait. And wait. And wait. Modelled this reaction for my son.

Kindness: Donated Girl Scout cookies to support our soldiers.

Goodness: Had a long conversation with a college student at the library.

Faith: Prayed hard for a sick family member.

Gentleness: Said no to a thoughtful invitation but did so in a sensitive, honest way.

Self-Control: Only ate one piece of dark chocolate when I preferred seven.

In addition to doing this reflection for ourselves, wouldn't this be an awesome way to ask the kids about their day? Rather than asking how their day went and getting a one-word answer, we could pull out a couple of Spirit virtues and chat about those instead: How were you loving today? How were you joyful today? How were you peaceful today? How were you patient today? How were you kind today? How were you good today? How were you faithful today? How were you gentle today? How did you show self-control today?

Embracing the fruit of Christ's Spirit as it spills out into our day is empowering. It's a bold reminder of our intrinsic ability to share His love when we allow His spirit to guide us.

Without changing the course of our daily interactions, continual whispers of goodness can become a booming case for kindness.

Deliberate kindness builds the strength of Christ's character within us. We receive His invitation to continually cultivate our rich soil, and through it, we welcome others to a banquet of sweet fruit!

We know how dearly God loves us, because he has given us the Holy Spirit to fill our hearts with his love.
ROMANS 5:5

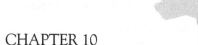

CHAPTER 10

LOVE THY NEIGHBOR

WE WERE THIRTY DAYS into our forty-day kindness commitment. We were still going strong and thoroughly enjoying our mission, but on this particularly crazy day, an act of kindness got lost in the chaos. My older son and I were driving home from an evening soccer practice when I suddenly realized I had missed a day. And it was late. Even the moon looked tired. It was time to go home and get everyone to bed (myself included).

As soon as I shared this predicament with my son, we spotted something at the exact same time. "Are you thinking what I'm thinking?" I asked. He nodded, and we pulled the car over, ready to slink into the night.

One house on the street (in addition to ours) still had garbage and recycling bins out by the road from trash collection that morning. Sneaking up to our friends' house, my son and I each grabbed a bin and quietly took it up the driveway, under the cover of darkness. We ran back to the car and raced away, laughing hysterically with our hearts pounding!

In a matter of minutes, we'd helped a neighbor, kept our chain of kindness going, and created a fun mother-son memory! *Jackpot.*

If I rewind about eight years, the same sweet boy, my partner in kindness, was a "spirited" toddler. (I think that's the friendly way to say "wild and driving everyone crazy.") Twice a week, I had to wake him from a much-needed nap so we could pick up his sister from preschool—a major bummer for him and for me.

One afternoon, my full-of-sunshine, Jesus-lovin', Texas-twangin' neighbor popped over just as I was plucking my little guy from a sound sleep to run out the door. From that day until the end of the school year, my cherished neighbor insisted that she work from my kitchen table for thirty minutes on those two days, so my son could keep sleeping. Total game changer. It's something I will never forget. Kindness.

Neighbors can be an unintended lifeline. They do life with us, traveling the same roads, watching our comings and goings, hearing the raised voices on our worst days when we forget the windows are open, sharing the corner of the world where God has us planted. With this proximity comes about a million opportunities for showing kindness.

We can help out when someone is away—get the mail, keep the fish alive, water the flowers. We can go out of our way to meet someone we don't know. Host a party. Start a book club, playgroup, or game night. Create a neighborhood website on nextdoor.com. We look out for one another: Invite a family to our holiday celebration when we know they will be alone. Mow, rake, or shovel. Tie balloons to a mailbox or front door for a birthday or new baby. Take our neighbor's dog for a walk. Be there to get the kids off the bus or meet a contractor when a friend is running late. Enlist others to help when there is a crisis or health concern. Be respectful. Organize a fun send-off before a move. Bring the newspaper up to the door, especially when there is an injury or bad weather. Stop over with something you baked or with dinner. Plan a movie night. Have a neighborhood no-charge, just-because lemonade stand.

Thinking about the blessings of neighbors nostalgically brings me back to the familiar streets of my hometown. My childhood neighborhood was up close and personal—simple ranch houses just a few paces from one another. Open doors. Conversations through windows. Endless bike rides and backyard baseball games. Driveway huddles that could last for hours. We never missed an opportunity to lend a hand. It was small-town living at its best.

One of our cherished neighbors found her way into our hearts through our stomachs. My brother Mark and I always knew when Mrs. Carney across the street was making her magical meatballs. The smell would waft across the road and into our bedroom windows. Without fail, we would head over to her house, and she would be ready with what we liked to call "meatball lollipops." She would answer our knock on her door with two forks in her hand, each boasting a plump, fried meatball. Glorious. Simple goodness in more than one way.

Memories of kindness that effortlessly endure the passing of time.

Whether an isolated gesture of compassion, a pervading atmosphere of love, or a weekly seat at the kitchen table, every extended hand is meaningful. Isn't it fascinating that in this great big world, our neighbors landed smack dab in the center of our daily grind? Where our paths may have never crossed with a different address, we now have a continual opening for connection. Kindness creates community, builds friendships, and amplifies the toasty warmth of home.

"'You must love the LORD your God with all your heart,
all your soul, all your mind, and all your strength.'
The second is equally important: 'Love your neighbor as yourself.'
No other commandment is greater than these."

MARK 12:30–31

CHAPTER 11

SELF-SERVE

WHEN I ACCEPTED the exciting opportunity to write this book, I was catapulted out of a decade-long gig as a stay-at-home mom. Elation and hesitation ran neck and neck, and I was hungry for advice on how to make all the pieces fit. I turned to my working-mom friends and cousins for advice, with a frequent go-to question: "What are your top three tips for balancing work and family?"

During my quest for guidance, there was one person I didn't even think of reaching out to—my own mom! Fortunately, moms have a way of knowing precisely what their children need, at any age.

One day, I opened my e-mail to find a detailed plan of action from the woman who, along with my dad, had worked from dawn to dusk to provide for our family. I can remember waking for school on dark, frigid Ohio mornings. Dad would already be on his long commute to work, but Mom would be zinging around the house in full gear, diligently getting things ready for the day. Her salon, Tina's Hair Design, was attached to our house, and I can't tell you how many times I heard her say when she picked me up from school or a sports practice, "We have to hurry; I'm in the middle of a perm!"

In her encouraging e-mail, my mom shared her experience and the importance of staying organized. She included some quick recipes and reminded me that the Crock-Pot is my friend. She suggested getting help with things I could delegate. She pointed out that kids benefit greatly from responsibility.

But her final paragraph stuck to me like a forgotten beef stew to the blasted Crock-Pot. A word of regret. A please-learn-from-my-mistakes. A silent wish for a do-over.

She told me very clearly to continue taking care of myself, to avoid meeting everyone's needs but my own. It's an incredibly valid point, and something we often overlook, regardless of how many balls we're trying to keep in the air.

Why is it so easy for us to put ourselves last? Perhaps we feel guilty claiming a piece of the limited time we have. Or maybe we sincerely believe we can't fit self-care into our endless list of tasks.

When we define or list acts of kindness, it is unusual to include showing love to our own bodies. Our own minds. Our own souls. And yet, if we allow ourselves to become depleted, we are unable to serve others. Unable to serve God.

In his book *Love: What Life Is All About,* Leo Buscaglia says it well: "One cannot give what he does not possess. To give love you must possess love. To love others you must love yourself." As we commit to transforming our mindsets to see, show, and celebrate kindness, let's also give generously to that awesome person in the mirror. We deserve it!

What kindness can we show ourselves? We can rediscover something we enjoy and prioritize time for it. Get enough sleep. Resist the urge to be endlessly productive. Don't be so hard on ourselves. Create something. Be still in the presence of God. Break a bad habit (one day at a time). Build a good habit (one day at a time). Breathe deeply. Read a good book. Begin a triumph journal, reflecting on our strengths and accomplishments each day. Take a walk with a friend. Start the day with a short Bible teaching on the First 5 app through Proverbs 31 Ministries. Try something new. Watch a funny movie and laugh hard. Enjoy the beauty of nature.

Many years ago, when my house was bustling with little people and I could see my most basic commitment to caring for myself starting to slip, I came up with something called my "Wellness Four-mula"—four nonnegotiables for my life. Four things I needed to protect and prioritize. Four things I could trust to get me back on track anytime I started to lose my way. My lighthouse. My stability bar.

Life has changed considerably since then, but my four things are still the same (and I'm still far from perfect at implementing them). My "four-mula" is:

- Get enough sleep,
- Take walks outside,
- Limit the amount of sugar I eat, and
- Commit to consistent time in prayer each day.

The last one, time in prayer, is my number one need. I must stay continually close to God, allowing His hand to guide me, or my very next turn could be directly into a wall. The words in Matthew 11:28–30 from *The Message* speak to me loud and clear; maybe they will resonate with you as well.

> Are you tired? Worn out? Burned out on religion? Come to me. Get away with me and you'll recover your life. I'll show you how to take a real rest. Walk with me and work with me—watch how I do it. Learn the unforced rhythms of grace. I won't lay anything heavy or ill-fitting on you. Keep company with me and you'll learn to live freely and lightly.

Yes. "Keep company with Me, and you'll learn to live freely and lightly."

Our lives require different types of fuel. Something that energizes you might exhaust someone else. But we can all find rest in God. And we all benefit greatly from showing love to ourselves, however that looks for each of us.

When we slow down and replenish, the time we invest in ourselves comes back to us ten time over! We are healthier, happier, more focused, more fulfilled. Our pursuit for kindness begins with the gifts of self-care and compassion. The more we pour into ourselves, the more we'll have to pour into the world.

---

*Dear friend, I hope all is well with you and that
you are as healthy in body as you are strong in spirit.*

3 John 1:2

CHAPTER 12

EXTRA MILE

IMAGINE YOU ARE WALKING briskly to your destination, minding your own business and going about your day, when you are approached by a person you despise. He hands you a heavy backpack (nearly one hundred pounds heavy!) and asks you to carry it for one mile . . . in the opposite direction of where you were heading. You will then have to walk a mile back to where you started! How might you respond to this request?

In Jesus's time, the Roman soldiers had taken over Israel. They were everywhere, even in the most sacred places. At any time, the soldiers were legally permitted to demand an able-bodied civilian to carry their armor for one mile. A dreaded obligation.

During Jesus's Sermon on the Mount, described in Matthew's gospel, He said something regarding this carry-my-stuff law that caused His followers to scrape their jaws off the ground. Jesus said,

"Whoever forces you to go one mile, go with him two" (Matthew 5:41 NASB).

Say what?

This behavior was unprecedented. Startling. Jesus was telling His disciples to go above and beyond their requirement, to give freely and generously from the heart, even when it wasn't deserved. I would have loved a peek at the soldiers' faces when they were offered that extra mile. By their nemesis! Their biggest question surely must have been, "Why?" The answer then—and the answer thousands of years later—is the same.

Jesus.

Jesus introduced a new way of thinking, a new attitude. His directive here originated the common phrase *go the extra mile*. He asks us to show love instead of affliction. To make an impact through unexplainable goodness. To show what it means to follow Him.

When it comes to helping others, the first mile typically doesn't make a loud boom; it is often expected or even required. But the extra mile? Ah, the extra mile is a head turner. A heart changer.

Our culture values immediacy. Quick. Easy. Now. Our check-it-off-the-list-and-move-on attitude can unfortunately spill into our interactions with others. When we're out in the world sprinkling kindness and sharing the heart of Jesus, let's be mindful of the joy and lasting impression of exceeding expectations.

We can drive out of our way to pick up a favorite treat for a friend. Hop on a plane to be there for a funeral, wedding, or special celebration. Rather than a quick hello or a wave, take time to get to know someone—give the gift of conversation. Send a care package.

Put our texting thumbs away and write an old-school letter with an envelope and a stamp! Create an "extra-mile" business strategy.

Often in our work, our volunteer positions, our relationships, and even in our homes, we are required to do things we may not enjoy. But we can take those obligations and turn them into opportunities for kindness, making the most of our "musts." When we must pack the kids' lunches, why not throw in a funny joke to brighten their day? When we must teach our Sunday school class, why not bring a fun treat to share? When we must attend a staff meeting, why not make a coffee run or pour drinks for our coworkers? When we must pick up our friends' mail, why not slip a thoughtful card into the pile . . . just because.

The unexpected nature of going above and beyond creates a lasting wow—like watching a fireworks display without knowing there will be a grand finale. The show seems great, and then . . . *wow*! Mind blown. Mouth gaping open.

Many years ago, I was visiting my brother on a small island in Lake Erie. We drove past his friend Mike's house and were surprised to see his red truck in the driveway. The previous night, he'd told us he had a big meeting in the city and he absolutely had to leave the island on the two o'clock ferry. When we asked what happened, he responded, "Well, I can go to work any day, it's not often you get to hang out with an awesome kid like Maggie."

Maggie was a sweet, seven-year-old girl with brown, curly pigtails and brilliant blue eyes. She wore cumbersome braces on both of her legs, bejeweled with purple and yellow stars. Maggie's family was visiting the island, and they happened to stop Mike for directions as he was heading to catch his boat. The island was very light on beaches, and that is precisely what they were in search of. Maggie's dad shared that he was hoping they could go to a beach while they were in town. It would be Maggie's first time, and she wanted to put her toes in the sand.

Mike let them know that he lived on the water and had a private beach that he would love to take them to. He cancelled his appointment and spent the afternoon with Maggie and her family. Toes in the sand—check! He even made a quick run to the grocery store so they could make gooey s'mores in the fire pit.

It certainly would have been expected for Mike to help Maggie's family, for him to give clear direction on the best place to go or even to have them follow him to a nearby beach. But this—this was no ordinary fireworks display. This was grand!

The first mile is an obligation. The extra mile is a beautiful offering, demonstrating the essence of God's love.

We know how much God loves us,
and we have put our trust in his love.
God is love, and all who live in love live in God,
and God lives in them.

1 JOHN 4:16

CHAPTER 13

ALL ABOUT BOOKS

MY HUSBAND AND I leisurely sifted through the glorious stacks of books in our favorite used bookstore. We were entranced by the fragrance of a wood-burning stove and a treasure of words around every narrow corner. Charming. Historic. Perfectly peaceful. Until a pack of wild children shook the ceiling above us and came barreling down the stairs. *Where in the world are their parents,* we wondered. Oh, right, that would be us!

Disruptively, our kids raced into the room, and I snarked, "What the heck? Are you guys crazy?" (Just as the parenting books on the shelves would recommend.)

They apologized between fits of laughter and revealed their urgent excitement. One of the kids asked if there were any gift cards and kindness cards in the car. They thought it would be awesome to slide a treasure into a random book in the store.

Our annoyance quickly vanished when we saw how jazzed they all were about an act of kindness! It was a true testimony to the power of forty *consecutive* days of kindness. Our kids were becoming independently and willingly engaged in spreading love.

Consistency creates habit. And what better habit to create than a loving heart and a generous hand?

We grabbed the supplies from our car: a kindness card and a $5 gift card to a favorite East Coast convenience shop. The kids slipped the items into an envelope and wrote: "Go ahead. Open it. Act of kindness enclosed. Have a nice day." And then we went about the task of finding the perfect book to hold the sweet surprise. I recommended the self-help section, thinking about the reaction of someone who might be looking for hope in a trying time. They ended up selecting *The Purpose Driven Life: What on Earth Am I Here For?* I think we were all starting to figure out the answer to that very question.

Over the next few weeks, our kids repeatedly asked to stop in the bookstore to see if anyone had found the loot, and eventually, it was discovered. Our kids beamed smiles, while another log was added to the growing flame of goodness.

Through this experience, we recognized the expansive value of books in spreading kindness. Here are a few simple ideas for sharing volumes of love: Make bookmarks out of card stock for library book returns. After finishing a good book, leave it on a bus seat or in a waiting room. Start a take-a-book, leave-a-book program at your church or at a local business—all you need is permission, a basket, a sign, and a few books to get started. When your Sunday school gets a new curriculum, donate gently used or unused materials to a local church in need. Reach out to your local library for donation opportunities. Read with a child. Create a homemade audiobook and send it to a long-distance family member or friend. Organize a book drive for a children's hospital, school, daycare, homeless shelter, or local prison, and slip notes of encouragement inside the books. Put a Bible in the hands of someone seeking Jesus at AmericanBible.org. Check out NationalLiteracyDirectory.org to find ways to support literacy in your own community. Support Reach Out and Read, ReachOutAndRead.org, a nonprofit organization providing millions of books to families through pediatric practices. Send books to soldiers through OperationPaperback.org. And maybe even share *A Case for Kindness* with a friend after you read it!

Even the littlest ones among us can tap into these suggestions to show love through books. Four-year-old Gracie was inspired during her family's Forty Days of Kindness journey. She was overjoyed by a basket of free books at a local toy store, and she wanted to share some of her books too.

As soon as she got home, she raced down to the basement and began embellishing an empty white box that had once held an arrangement of fresh flowers. When the box was delightfully decorated with bright red hearts and three butterfly stickers, she wrote the words: FREE BOOKS . . . with a backward R and a smiley face in one of the O's. Then she filled the box with some of her books and placed it on her front porch. She and her mom set out to spread the word in their neighborhood, and sweet Gracie was glowing with pride.

After Gracie created her book box, her parents began to hear about the nonprofit Little Free Library (LittleFreeLibrary.org). This organization increases access to books all around the world with free book exchanges. Anyone can take a book or leave one to share. The charming wooden "little libraries" come in different shapes and sizes, and there are over fifty thousand of them registered throughout seventy countries. With contributions through their Impact Fund, the organization also donates little libraries to communities where they can make a big difference. Such a fantastic way for masses of people to discover the great truth behind Walt Disney's words: "There is more treasure in books than all the pirates' loot on Treasure Island."

Just like the bound beauties overflowing our favorite bookstore shelves and libraries both big and little, avenues for kindness surround us. When we commit *to daily* acts of love, these opportunities start flying off the pages, and we become increasingly motivated to discover and deliver on kindness.

Repetition reaps great rewards—it's the perfect reason to run wild with excitement.

So, my dear brothers and sisters, be strong and immovable.
Always work enthusiastically for the Lord,
for you know that nothing you do for the Lord is ever useless.
1 CORINTHIANS 15:58

CHAPTER 14

LET GOD LEAD

I STOOD IMPATIENTLY in the grocery store line, holding a colorful bouquet of flowers. My daughter's performance was beginning shortly, and I was anxious to get to the theater.

Even in my haste, I couldn't help but notice the family directly behind me. Very gently, the dad spoke to his children as they casually leaned on their mom's wheelchair. He examined the contents of the shopping cart and quietly commented that they needed to put a few things back.

With an urgency in my soul beyond words, I instinctively grabbed a gift card off the shelf and added it to my order. Discreetly, I set the card on top of their cereal box as it glided down the conveyer belt. And I slipped out of the store.

Heart racing, eyes full, I got in my car and just sat there, overwhelmed. *This*, I thought, *is the meaning behind "God's work. Our hands."* The action alone was nothing remarkable, but the force behind the action was not mine. That was clear.

In writing this book, I looked back at the journal I'd kept throughout my forty-day kindness celebration, and I found these words: "No doubt this was bigger than I could ever be on my own. I felt God's hand in that moment, and I was so thankful to have been present to see His goodness."

Do you ever feel a similar stirring, a nudge from within, drawing you toward another person? Perhaps it's a simple thought to reach out to a friend with a phone call or text. Maybe you've sensed a sudden urge to volunteer in your community or help someone in need.

It's easy for us to push aside those heart tugs. We may sincerely intend to follow through, then life gets in the way and we don't get around to it. A sermon from a visiting preacher drove this message home, leading off with the words of Oscar Wilde: "The smallest act of kindness is worth more than the grandest intention." The pastor encouraged us to "just do it" whenever we feel moved to reach out to another person, even if it is simply sending a card. Those persistent prods are courtesy of the Holy Spirit, seeking the work of our hands, urging us to act. I can't say I have ever regretted obediently responding with compassion, but I have also dropped the ball after feeling that call to action—and wished deeply that I had made the time to follow through.

In many situations, the whispers from the Holy Spirit require swift action, but sometimes they require patience.

I was feeling God's undeniable nudges toward a struggling

woman in my community. I barely knew her, but I couldn't shake continual thoughts of her. Since our paths rarely crossed and it wasn't a situation where I could just make an awkward phone call, I was at a loss for what to do.

So I prayed.

I prayed for her every day. And I trusted that if I was to do more, God would sort out the details of an encounter.

Many weeks passed and nothing happened; I started to question if I had mistakenly assumed God's hand was involved.

And then I saw her at the farmer's market.

Rather than just saying hello and going about my business, I took a deep breath and walked over to her. With immediate gratitude for the chance to reach out, I mentioned her place in my prayers . . . and her eyes filled with tears. She shared that just that morning, she had reached her breaking point.

Just that morning, she needed a word of encouragement.

Just that morning, she needed a reminder that she wasn't alone.

Just that morning, she needed to know God had not forgotten about her.

Just that morning! Amazed.

What a gift to see the Holy Spirit at work, right there next to the arugula and the precut celery.

So often we question God's presence and His timing. We can dismiss that still, small voice, thinking He couldn't possibly want to use us in His plan. But we are all needed, and He has the details worked out. Lysa TerKeurst says it well, "Our job is to be obedient to God; God's job is everything else."

As we seek to make kindness reflexive, our most valuable

strategy is to let God lead. When we accept those nudges as the Holy Spirit speaking directly to our hearts, we will be more likely to put feet to our intentions. We will witness firsthand the living power of God's Word that is "sharper than any double-edged sword . . . ; it judges the thoughts and attitudes of the heart" (Hebrews 4:12 NIV).

The perfect place to begin seeking God's guidance for our kindness mission is in prayer, remembering the importance of silence so we can hear His voice within us. We can ask Him each morning to direct our paths. Lead us to where we are needed. Show us how to make a difference. Fill us with a hunger to serve. Give us confidence to be bold.

Then, with open eyes and willing hearts, we will feel Him moving in our lives. Working through us. Drawing us closer to Him. Teaching us to live like Jesus. For Jesus.

Show me the right path, O LORD;
point out the road for me to follow.
Lead me by your truth and teach me,
for you are the God who saves me.
All day long I put my hope in you.

PSALM 25:4–5

CHAPTER 15

PEOPLE BEFORE PROJECTS

THE DATE ON THE CALENDAR was taunting me. I quickly diverted my eyes, as if the deadline would disappear if I didn't look.

Zoned out. Head in my hands. . . . I felt a tap on my shoulder. I looked up to see my daughter Ellie, her eyes filled with tears.

We had known for months that one of her closest friends was moving to France. But on this day, she learned that the departure date had been expedited. Her cherished BFF was leaving the following week.

Heartbreak.

The question on the table left me with wide eyes and labored breathing, "Can we have a big going-away party for her this weekend?"

Oh, man. I wanted to. Of course I wanted to. I just couldn't pull it off that weekend, I told her. I was so sorry, but I had way too much work to do.

She understood, hoping someone else could host the party. But I knew she was disappointed; it was written all over her face.

The next morning, after a sleepless night and a serious priority check, I went to my daughter with an apology and a changed answer. Essentially, what I told her the previous day was, "I don't have time for you and your friends because I'm entirely too busy writing a book about kindness!"

Ouch. Staring at the truth can be painful. And this certainly wasn't the first time I'd chosen completion over connection. Particularly as caregivers, we can find ourselves in a constant tug-of-war between doing things *for* our people and doing things *with* them—often prioritizing tedious tasks over treasured time.

Shortly after this wake-up call, I had the privilege of hearing speaker Jill Savage, founder of Hearts at Home, address the challenge of putting first things first. She said three words that are now etched on my heart: "people before projects."

People before projects.

As we seek to balance the demand of our responsibilities with the opportunity of our blessings, this simple phrase can give us perspective. It reminds us where true value is found and challenges the assumption that productivity is the ultimate measure of success. And it offers a formula for rest and renewal.

Throughout the course of a day, chances to choose people over projects abound. We can drop what we're doing when a friend needs a hand. Say "yes" instead of "wait a minute." Put down our phones and be present. Forget the dirty dishes and take a family walk after dinner. Show forgiveness in the face of a time-consuming error. We can give our client, student, employee, or patient extra time, even when we're swamped. Take time to pray with our kids at the end of an exhausting day. Answer the phone when we know the call may take a while.

We can enjoy our houseguests, even when dust bunnies adorn the kitchen floor. Enjoy our family during the holidays, even if we only made half of the cookies we had planned. Enjoy the people we get to do life with, even when the to-do list runneth over.

Have you ever been on the receiving end of this equation, knowing someone was putting you before a task they needed to complete? There is something incredibly filling in the words, "It can wait."

On the flip side, if you have ever felt dismissed for the sake of a project, you know that feeling is just as sticky. It tends to hang around and fester. I can recall a day many years ago when I was in a huge bind, desperately seeking a helping hand. I reached out to a friend and she said she was sorry, but she was just about to run out to the fruit market.

Okay, I'm a big fan of fruit too. But to me, this seemed like something that could wait.

Don't get me wrong; I don't expect people to jump the minute I beckon for aid. And I know that sometimes there is more than meets the eye. Maybe this was the only moment in an overwhelming week to sneak away and restock her house. Maybe she was having guests for dinner. But the possible reason didn't change the way her response affected me. I hung up the phone with my heart in my stomach. I felt pushed aside, disappointed.

Our actions, whether attentive or inattentive, carry megaphone messages to the people in our lives. When we put people first, we fill them up with memorable, life-giving words. *You are worth it. You are valued. You are important. You are loved.*

Acts of kindness aren't rooted solely in what we do; the transformative piece of the kindness puzzle often begins with the way we make someone feel. We can use our gifts of time and selflessness to feed the soul of another person and, at the same time, leave a lasting impression of Christ's love.

And that's a mission far more pressing than any deadline.

Teach us to realize the brevity of life,
so that we may grow in wisdom.
PSALM 90:12

CHAPTER 16

PHOTO OP

DELETE. DELETE. DELETE. WAIT! Bombarded with junk e-mails, I was happy to see a dear friend's name—Peg.

"Found this in my draft file," she began. I curiously opened the attachment. My little family looked right at me, as if I had walked into another lifetime! The kids were tiny—toys in hands, cake frosting on shirts. We all wore glowing smiles on our faces, coupled with delirious exhaustion for me and my husband. The image was like a time machine. Memories flooded from a precious season in our lives, gone in a blink yet forever present.

The power of a photograph.

An unrivaled treasure.

With a big heart, a great camera, and a keen eye, Peg has created a personal kindness ministry, photographing and presenting everyday life and once-in-a-lifetime moments. Special celebrations. Concerts. Weddings. Baptisms. Funerals. Senior center events. Christmas pageants. Neighborhood gatherings. Service projects. Wherever people gather together, she is there. Preserving smiles and tears. Pressing pause so we can stay a little longer, so we can look a little more closely. On a mission of love, she embraces God's gifts, replicating His image as she captures ours.

Fortunately, the art of memory making is something we can enjoy too, with just a little creativity and an attentive spirit. With today's technology, cameras are often handy in our pockets. We can stop time with more ease than ever, uniquely creating smiles from smiles and continuing to spread kindness.

We can capture tender, candid moments for our loved ones and send them the pictures. Two of my kids went to a festival with friends of ours many years ago, and as the kids walked around, they held hands. My thoughtful friend snapped a quick photo of them from behind and texted it to me. In one second, she'd created a gift that I will cherish always.

We can make a "Happy Birthday" video . . . sing it loud and proud! Offer to go to a friend's house or a park to take their family photo. Use a great picture from a friend's social media page to make them a photo gift or frame. Gather photos of someone who has passed and share them with the grieving family. Take seasonal pictures of a neighbor's house or a favorite tree and make a photo collage. When we have a front-row seat at a kids' concert or show, we can snag a few shots of our friends' children too.

We can make a photo board or an online photo book after an event or at the end of a sports season. I always sincerely appreciate the parents with great cameras who take action shots of all the kids and then make a group Snapfish or Shutterfly album of a classroom, a team, or a performance. They always seem to capture something that I missed or fill in the gap from extreme photo slacking.

We can offer to jump in as the photographer for strangers, so nobody is left out of the picture. Photograph a child's artwork each year and turn it into a photo book. Send a handwritten note with the hard copy of a meaningful photo. Create a slideshow of photos to loop at a special event. Send a "throwback" picture to a friend on a random day . . . just because. Never miss the chance to take a multigenerational picture! Splurge on a portrait studio gift card for a new baby. Decorate a plain wooden craft frame with festive scrapbooking stickers, insert photo, and give as a gift. Celebrate a birthday or anniversary with pictures through the years.

My sister-in-law, Melissa, is committed to making a photo calendar every year, and she gives them as Christmas gifts. This project is a huge undertaking, as she includes pictures of all the extended family. She reaches out to us every fall to ask if we have any favorite pictures we want her to include. She highlights everyone's birthday and anniversary and documents them with photos, leaving no excuse to forget to call on the special day. The archived calendars through the years are timeless treasures.

With a single glance, photos can move us to laughter or tears, reviving forgotten times and leaving imprints of our life story. Like a camera dangling close to the heart of the photographer, may we carry kindness with us wherever we go, tapping into its astonishing power to make a lasting impression.

Never let loyalty and kindness leave you!
Tie them around your neck as a reminder.
Write them deep within your heart.

PROVERBS 3:3

CHAPTER 17

TRASH OR TREASURE

I REACHED HIGH and into the depths of an overflowing cabinet. Suddenly, an unfamiliar object shot out, ricocheted off my head, and bounced across the worn hardwood floor. *Ouch. What in the world was that thing?* I glanced down to see Elmo's friendly face staring at me. I couldn't help but smile back. Until I realized I was looking at a sippy cup . . . and my youngest child was in first grade!

The house had gotten out of hand; it was bursting at the seams with stuff. Much of it no longer served a purpose. Some of it had *never* served a purpose. That clunk to the head was just the jolt I needed to get my act together.

I made a plan to ransack the place. Over the next few months, I took it one room at a time and sifted through everything. Every closet. Every cabinet. Every dresser. Every nightstand. Every storage bin. Every toy. Every holiday decoration. Everything. I touched every single stinkin' thing in the house, assessing the contents as if we were moving to Timbuktu.

And it was painfully marvelous!

And through this extreme purging process, I received as much as I removed.

Freedom. Clarity. Space. Time. I humbly and imperfectly started to see that less is often more, and *enough* is a powerful word. I embraced and more fully enjoyed the things that made the cut. Things that were loved or useful to my family.

The sprinkles on the sundae came as I made plans for the surplus. For all the excess we see or experience, there is a greater amount of need. For every too much, there is a too little. For every clearing out, there is a welcoming in.

Letting go of the extras in our lives and sharing what we no longer use can profoundly impact others right in our community or across the globe.

My friend, Amy, got a front-row seat to this impact when she delivered two car seats to a local day shelter. When she brought her donations to the shelter, the woman at the desk was moved to tears. She said there were families in enormous need of car seats right then, and before Amy was even out the door, she heard the excited phone call sharing the good news with a family. Amy was so touched by this, she turned around and asked about other items that would be helpful for their current families. Then she sent an e-mail to a group of friends (anyone with baby items collecting dust and spiders in our basements) requesting help to meet the needs. It was a much-needed reminder that just because we're not using something doesn't mean it can't be used.

Whether we have many items to donate or just one, looking locally is a perfect way to begin when seeking a happy home for our goods. Reach out to schools, churches, animal shelters, food banks, libraries, charity stores, prisons, senior centers, halfway houses, nursing homes, and day-care centers. Contact local youth athletic organizations, dance schools, and music studios—some kids could greatly benefit from gently used gear, equipment, and instruments. Ask the local fire station if they accept stuffed animals. Create a relationship with a less-privileged school or church; this provides a wonderful opportunity for one community to help another community throughout the entire year with school supplies, holiday gifts, winter coats, food, books, and most importantly . . . hope.

With so much focus on the darkness in our world, it is astounding to see the radiant light that is spreading across the globe. Philanthropic organizations abound, ready to utilize us and put our unwanted items into thankful hands.

If you want to learn more about specific nonprofit organizations before donating or volunteering, websites like guidestar.org and greatnonprofits.org are valuable resources.

Here are a few reliable organizations that are happy to turn trash into treasure. Some, like the Salvation Army at SAtruck.org or the Military Order of the Purple Heart at purpleheartpickup. org will even pick up your donations. Send eyeglasses to the Lion's Club at LionsClub.org. Get rid of those old prom dresses and help a teen have a night to remember at GlassSlipperProject.org. Empower victims of domestic violence by donating cell phones to the National Coalition against Domestic Violence at NCADV.org.

Check with local libraries and colleges about opportunities to unload used computers; many have a relationship with World Computer Exchange. Large electronic retail stores often have collection events for safe recycling as well.

Donations also offer a great way to get others involved in giving, and they multiply the amount of goods we have to share. We can let our neighborhood know that we're collecting gently used backpacks for the new school year and put a bin out in our driveway. Organize a winter coat drive or a bike drive at our kids' school. Adopt a family at Christmas with a Bible study group, book club, or sports team. Involve coworkers in the annual Men's Warehouse National Suit Drive; this event benefits at-risk men and women seeking to enter or reenter the workforce (menswarehouse.com— enter "suit drive" in the search box).

While we may not think we are well connected, we all have people in our lives we can call upon for doing good works. Chances are, they will be happy to help!

Eleven-year-old Hannah invited her friends to help others as part of her birthday celebration. Four months after her kindness project ended, Hannah decided to ask for donations instead of gifts at her party. She asked her friends to bring supplies for a local food bank, and she was overwhelmed by the response. When asked about her choice to pass up getting presents, her answer was, "I know people need things more than I do."

Thinking through our stuff and recognizing our opportunities to give generously helps us to fully comprehend the vast expanse of need around us. When we increase our awareness and decrease our accumulation, we can help others survive and thrive while freeing ourselves of excess in the process. It's the ultimate win-win.

All must give as they are able, according to the blessings given to them by the LORD your God.

DEUTERONOMY 16:17

CHAPTER 18

FREEDOM IN FORGIVENESS

I WAS BROWSING THE VIDEOS in our church library, when a friend picked a DVD off the shelf and handed it to me.

"Watch this," she said. "You'll never be the same. Make sure to have a box of tissues nearby."

Hesitantly, I took the movie from her, feeling a pang of resistance as I saw the title, *Amish Grace*. I remembered seeing this heart-wrenching story on the news back in 2006. My daughter was now close in age to the ten girls who'd faced the unimaginable—a murderous gunman in their serene Amish schoolhouse. I gave myself the usual pep talk, the one I often use as I struggle through a book or movie based on distressful true events. I remind myself that people actually endured the tragedy; the least I can do is hear their story and allow their pain to find purpose as it ministers to others.

My friend was right. Long after the credits rolled, this soul-reaching message of forgiveness continued to echo. Courageous forgiveness. Like never before. Amid the most devastating offense conceivable, the grieving families chose to forgive. They reached out to the family of the man who shattered their lives, refusing to allow hatred into their hearts. They demonstrated that faith is an action—not a cluster of words or a set of beliefs tossed aside when life gets ugly.

Forgiveness doesn't mean acceptance; it doesn't mean absolution. It means removing the shackles that will keep us from moving forward. Forgiveness might not heal a relationship, but it will heal our hearts. Choosing to forgive is a gift to ourselves, a gift of freedom, a gift of restoration. Conversely, hanging on to hatred and resentment binds us and leads us away from love, away from kindness, away from Christ.

One of my boys had an upsetting interaction with a good friend at school that ultimately required a silent offering of forgiveness. His friend didn't realize how much hurt his actions had caused my son, and there was no apology or remorse in sight.

With mounting frustration and gloom pulling him down, our mornings became a battle to get him out the door for school. Soon enough, the resistance increased, and tension started building at bedtime for the following day. Stress, bitterness, and anger spewed from his little body.

I even started to see changes in his behavior and his overall attitude. At dinner, we like to go around the table (when we make it to the table) and share our "Yays, Nays, and Prays"—one high for the day, one low for the day, and one prayer. This kid was always the king of the double yay, frequently sharing two yays because he couldn't think of a nay! But during these days of angst, there was scarcely a yay to be found. His nays were front and center. His inability to let go of this transgression was crushing him, and a dark cloud followed wherever he went.

Just as I was feeling like I needed to figure out a better plan to help, I saw a lightness emerge. Finally, he started bolting out the door again for school. Eventually, he even began speaking positively about his friend. I talked to my son about the change I was seeing, and asked him if something had happened to make things better. An apology? A conversation? A nice gesture from his friend?

"Nothing happened," he answered. "I'm just not letting it bother me so much anymore."

He decided to let go and move forward, and he instantly started to feel better. This entire process occurred without any involvement from the other child. Forgiveness happened inside my son's heart. It was about him. It was about no longer allowing resentment to gnaw away at him and take away his yays. Only he had the power to release those feelings and find his way back to peace.

Liberation through forgiveness extends beyond what we provide for ourselves and for others when we are hurt. Great benefits come through forgiving ourselves, asking forgiveness, and accepting forgiveness from God and from others. Of course, one thing is clear across the board: it is hard! Engaging in the work of forgiveness requires much, but the harvest is abundant.

If there's a weight you're carrying and these words are resonating with you, maybe an act of forgiveness would be the perfect blessing for your kindness journey.

Writing can be an exceptional first step when navigating the fitful sea of forgiveness. We can brainstorm what we want to say before offering or seeking forgiveness. Take out some paper and pour out the story—raw emotions are welcome! Try journaling, splattering negative thoughts onto paper so they don't swallow us up. We can write a letter we don't intend to send to the offending person—while the words won't be received, the writing process can open a door to healing.

We can use small pieces of paper to write down the feelings and circumstances we wish to release, then drop the papers into a fireplace or a shredder. We can hang a sticky note on the bathroom mirror declaring "Freedom in Forgiveness," and be reminded that hanging onto negative feelings won't change the situation or help in any way. Keep moving toward release. Practice writing or saying the words, "I forgive you," or "Will you forgive me?" And when we're ready, if it's realistic to do so, we can take a courageous step toward the person we seek to forgive or from whom we seek forgiveness.

When we clutch unforgiveness, we seal off the entrance to our hearts, unintentionally posting a "Keep Out" sign for love and peace. Life is too short, too sacred, to be consumed by bitterness and discord. Let's choose forgiveness. We have the most to gain!

Be kind to each other, tenderhearted, forgiving one another, just as God through Christ has forgiven you.

EPHESIANS 4:32

CHAPTER 19

THE OPPOSITE OF A BAD GUY

AFTER A LONG, FRIGID WINTER, the calendar finally flipped to March 20. The first day of spring! Time to thaw out.

We were in high gear with Forty Days of Kindness, so we decided to celebrate big.

"Happy Spring! Help yourself to the toys." The embellished sign put the final touch on a shiny red crate overflowing with all things outdoor fun: bubbles, sidewalk chalk, parachute guys, jump ropes, mini kick balls, Wiffle ball sets, and Frisbees.

Our master plan was to drop the bin of toys at a local park, all stealthy and unnoticed, then hightail it back to our cool getaway car. (Okay, it was a minivan. Whatever.)

My little kindness buddy, Charlie, beamed with anticipation, thrilled that his half-day kindergarten schedule left him wide open for these exhilarating missions with Mom.

We designated the perfect drop spot, swiftly delivered the goods, and sped back to the car with red faces and thumping chests. Still bouncing with joy as he buckled his seatbelt, Charlie looked up and declared with elation, "I feel like the opposite of a bad guy!"

Clarity washed over me in that moment, and I felt overwhelming gratitude for this simple project. Undeniably, a message of love was seeping directly into the hearts of my kids.

These "sneaky" acts of kindness are fun for all ages! What a thrill to leave something behind, knowing we could brighten another person's day. And the best part is—since we don't see what happens next—it's all about the action, not the reaction.

We can attach a bag of coins to a parking meter or vending machine. Create a Laundromat care package filled with quarters, snacks, and magazines. Add some excitement to a children's waiting room with a new activity or toy. Tape a dollar bill to the back of a bag of chips or a candy bar. Sneak a treat onto a coworker's desk. Surprise a friend with a potted plant on their front porch. Slip a gift card and kindness card into the pocket of a new coat at the mall. Decorate someone's locker or door for their birthday. Leave a few stamps on the post office prep table. Clip coupons and put them next to the corresponding products in the store.

These random, secret-service style acts of love that could end up in just about anyone's hands are filled with opportunity. God can jump right in to complete the equation when we walk away. We can even say a quick prayer as we leave something behind, asking for that small sprinkling of glitter to land precisely where it was meant to be. So it becomes a glimmer of hope, a reminder of goodness in the world. Perfect timing to satisfy a need.

Clandestine acts of kindness can also be undercover without being random. In other words, they are still done in secret but are very much directed toward a particular person.

A struggling family with small children was dealing with a devastating loss. Their story had been in the local news, so the situation was well known in their small community. They opened their mailbox one day to find an anonymous package that held tickets to Disney on Ice, spending money for the event, and a gift card to a restaurant.

A beloved bus driver named Ruth was battling severe depression, and she was unable to find light. On a particularly desperate day, she heard a knock on her door. When she answered, nobody was there. Then she looked down to find an enormous, stunning vase filled with vibrant flowers. She opened the card, and it said: "I love you. Jesus." Ruth never did find out who sent the flowers. Friend or stranger, it didn't really matter. It came from somebody's heart to lift her spirit and remind her that she was loved. Always. And it brought a recently unfamiliar expression to her face. A smile.

Spreading love behind a curtain of anonymity is an engaging way to find the spirit of kindness. When we remove the possibility of receiving credit for our actions, the act gains a special purity; an altruism that is not lost on the receiver. It also allows us to extend a hand in circumstances that might otherwise cause hesitation.

As seen in Charlie's reaction, kids are especially fueled by undercover kindness. They are drawn to its super-hero charm, and it's a fun way to introduce them to the joy of focusing on others.

When I think about the adults I want my children to become, I'm feeling pretty darn good about being "the opposite of a bad guy." What better way to lead them, and ourselves, down that path than through selflessness? Giving for the sake of giving; loving simply because we were loved first.

Give your gifts in private, and your Father,
who sees everything, will reward you.
MATTHEW 6:4

CHAPTER 20

FAITHFUL FRIEND

OVERWHELMED. TEARS STREAMING. I couldn't believe this was happening again. And I was starting to panic. Who would have guessed that a back injury so long ago would keep visiting me, wreaking havoc on our lives. No bending or lifting. Yeah. Tell that to a toddler and two preschoolers.

Slowly and cautiously, my husband helped me into the house, and I was immediately drawn to a burst of color on the cluttered kitchen counter.

Flowers.

And a lasagna!

I wasn't even sure how my friend knew I was out of commission (or how she got into the house), but she didn't waste any time springing into action. A note on top of our dinner included baking directions, a declaration that she would be taking the kids the next day, and a brilliant glimmer of hope that I might just make it through this setback with some sanity intact.

Ah, friends and family. What an incredible difference they can make when we're struggling.

Whether we care to admit it or not, life is filled with challenges and hardship. Sometimes it stinks. But the tough times present glorious opportunities for us to show up with compassion.

When a friend needs a hand because of an illness or injury, a death in the family, a new baby, an ailing child or parent, a difficult loss, or simply a bad day, we are privileged to deliver a ray of hope. What looks like a chicken casserole or an encouraging card is actually a sacred reminder that we are not alone. Someone noticed. Someone cares. Someone will lighten the load.

Do you ever genuinely desire to provide this relief for others, but stumble over where to start? Me too. And sometimes my result is great intentions without any follow through.

Thinking back to that desperate day, what I appreciated most about my concerned friend was her boldness. She acted immediately and had a plan for how to help. If she had said, "Give me a call if you need help with dinner or the kids," there is a good chance I would have decided not to bother her, even knowing she was sincere in her offer.

When we're seeking to reach out to friends or family members in a bind, being specific is key. Ask what time you can stop over to walk the dog. Let them know you're going to mow their lawn on Mondays. Call to say you're bringing dinner tomorrow and ask what they're in the mood for. Drop a quick text from the grocery store and ask what they need. Take their carpool shift indefinitely.

Set up a standing day to watch the kids, drive them to an appointment, or help with laundry. Enlist others to help with meals—check out MealTrain.com or TakeThemAMeal.com. And sometimes it's enough to just be there. Just *be* there.

Within the reality of our ultra busy lives, and perfect for friends who need some space, there are also effective ways to reach out from home or even from our phones. Add them to a prayer chain or a prayer list. Make a fun video—include the kids or the family pet. E-mail or text an encouraging Bible verse (Isaiah 41:10 is a winner: "Don't be afraid, for I am with you. Don't be discouraged, for I am your God. I will strengthen you and help you. I will hold you up with my victorious right hand.") Send a card or a piece of artwork. Call them and listen intently. Ask for their input on how to help. And most importantly, pray, pray, and then pray! And let them know you are praying.

These opportunities to care for others bring us blessing in our role as the giver. In Acts 20:35, the apostle Paul says: "And I have been a constant example of how you can help those in need by working hard. You should remember the words of the Lord Jesus: 'It is more blessed to give than to receive.'" With these words in mind, we have the chance to bless others by *asking* for help. We can provide an avenue to kindness.

It can be quite difficult to reach out from a place of need and ask for a loving hand, but embracing the benefits for the giver can decrease our hesitance. By offering a way for someone to help when they might not otherwise consider it, we are giving them the gifts of being a giver. Gifts that include joy, perspective, awareness, fulfillment, and inspiration.

We are all called to love one another as God loves us (John 13:34). Love. Love as an action. Love as a commitment. When we go out of our way to share the burdens of others, to stand with them in the darkness, we are demonstrating the love of Christ, fulfilling the very purpose of our lives.

A friend is always loyal,
and a brother is born to help in time of need.
PROVERBS 17:17

CHAPTER 21

WHAT'S IN A NAME?

I TURNED THE CORNER on my morning walk, and there she was . . . just like yesterday and the day before. A fit woman in a pink baseball cap with a quick, peppy stride. We passed each other often and waved, even commented occasionally about the weather. On this morning, however, I was spontaneously inspired to stop and ask her name. Why not? Midway through my forty days of kindness, I was hyperfocused on really seeing the people in my path, and I was sincerely interested in her answer.

She may have thought I was crazy at first, but as she walked away with a smile, I knew she'd appreciated the thoughtful gesture.

Moving forward, a new comfort emerged in our morning greetings. Simply using our first names had created a connection. A certain familiarity between us. Undeniably, being called by name is like a spoken hug, covering us with a spirit of caring and warmth.

In his book *How to Win Friends and Influence People*, author Dale Carnegie puts it this way, "A person's name is to that person the sweetest and most important sound in any language." Taking the time to ask and then retain a person's name gives us the opportunity to produce that sacred sound.

Easy enough, right? Not exactly. Can you relate to forgetting someone's name *while* being introduced to them? Like, immediately? I've done this more than once, and I always kick myself and wish I had a rewind button.

Seeking to be more mindful of this frustrating tendency of mine, I've discovered a few useful remedies. First, knowing that remembering a name is important encourages attentive listening. Once I've deliberately absorbed the name, I find it tremendously helpful to use it again right away. My brain seems to enjoy (or require) this more and more as I get older!

It's also extremely effective to make a mental image of the new person standing beside a friend with the same name. You'll be surprised at how well this strategy will help you bring up the image and access the name. Finally, don't be afraid to ask again. It's better to ask for a refresher sooner rather than five encounters later when it's downright awkward.

Once we've mastered remembering names, we can practice this skill in all kinds of fantastic ways, strengthening relationships and, of course, sprinkling kindness.

Begin by learning the names of the people we see regularly in our community: a postal worker, the bus driver, a custodian, the security officer at work, staff members at church and school, the barista at the coffee shop. This small effort can begin many happy exchanges and even foster friendships, where we once would have allowed people to remain nameless. Invisible. Just walking right past every day.

My family was joining friends for dinner at their favorite seafood restaurant. We jumped online to look at the menu. While there, we stumbled upon multiple reviews, and the comments were exceptional—except for a surprising number of people mentioning one notably grumpy waiter! "The biggest crab in the entire place," a customer exclaimed.

When we walked into the restaurant, one of the servers made a beeline for our friends. And they were as happy to see each other as long-lost pals at a class reunion. *Such a sweet relationship*, I thought, as we headed to our table. As we sat down, lobster artichoke dip already on its way out, we asked them to point out the notoriously cranky waiter in the restaurant. Following a burst of laughter, they shared that it was their friend; the one they had just greeted!

Penetrating his grouchy exterior and finding an ultra soft heart had been simple. Many years earlier, their daughter asked him his name. His name is Bernard. She made the effort to see him and to know him. It made all the difference.

Being mindful of the value in learning names will reveal a variety of great opportunities. We can help new people feel welcome by using their names frequently. Create fun ways for groups of children to learn one another's names. Call local business owners by name. As a business owner, seek to learn your customers' names. We can ask for the names of homeless people in our communities, then call them by name every chance we get. And we can pray for others by name.

Our congregation fiercely adored Pastor Bill. He was masterful at learning names. He worked hard at this undertaking; it was a priority. And it was extremely effective in building relationships. Even when he distributed communion, he would call us by name. We weren't just more faces in a large sea of people. Learning our names created a connection and caused us to be more likely to reach out to him in times of need as well as joy. This same effect holds true in settings like workplaces and classrooms—it makes the atmosphere feel smaller and the people more familiar, more approachable.

Learning and using names is not typically thought of as an act of kindness, yet it is a key ingredient in building friendly communities. So let's grab our "Hello, My Name Is" badges and head on out to greet the world. One name at time.

Do not be afraid, for I have ransomed you.
I have called you by name; you are mine.

ISAIAH 43:1

CHAPTER 22

MAY I
HAVE A WORD?

TRYING TO IGNORE the internal rant spinning through my head, I approached the all-too-familiar maroon door. *How many stinkin' times am I going to do this? What makes this umpteenth attempt any different? Maybe I should just turn around and get out of here—I'll start next month.*

With an already defeated attitude and a list of about 107 other things I would rather be doing on a Saturday morning, I hauled my sorry buns to the Weight Watchers meeting. Again.

As I stood in the entrance of the office complex, I noticed an abandoned bulletin board. The display was completely empty, aside from one iridescent sticker shimmering the words "You are beautiful."

You are beautiful.

Three simple words. Immeasurable impact.

I have no idea who lovingly bejeweled the board, but right then I'd desperately needed to receive that message. And I was grateful. Grateful for the gift of thoughtfulness. Grateful for the reminder that we are all beautiful in God's eyes. Always.

I walked into that weekly meeting with a glimmer of hope, taking a step back from self-inflicted shame and disappointment and a step closer to success and good health.

All around us, people are tearing each other down by the spewing of negative words. But words can be used just as powerfully to build each other up. We all have the capacity to relay Christ's love through the words we share each day.

And the opportunities are all around us!

One of my favorite ways to do this is by telling a manager that an employee was awesome. We can be quick to complain when someone is doing a lousy job; how about when they knock it out of the park? Sharing that someone did an exceptional job is a special way to say "you rock," and it may end up benefitting them with their employer.

A member of the housekeeping staff at a hotel, Maria, inspired me to seek out a manager to sing her praises. She was just finishing her work when I returned to the room with one of my kids who was feeling sick. We made small talk with her for a few minutes, and after she left I settled my little one into bed for a nap. A few minutes later, I heard a light tap on the door, and Maria was there with juice, crackers, and an extra blanket. As if that wasn't kind enough, the next day when she came to the room, she left a sweet note and three little stuffed animals for the kids.

Maria provided a beautiful example of the words in Colossians 3:23: "Work willingly at whatever you do, as though you were working for the Lord rather than for people."

Before we left the hotel, I made sure to talk to a manager about the above and beyond attention we received. The manager shared how thankful she was for the feedback, as the hotel often selected its employees of the month through positive customer reviews.

The opportunities for blessing others with our words certainly don't stop there. We can send a "just because you're amazing" letter to a friend. Acknowledge colleagues for their hard work. Put a note of praise in a child's lunchbox. Use a dry-erase marker to write a love note on our significant other's mirror or even on the car window. Give a sincere compliment. Stand up for the underdog. Stock up on Bibles, highlight some of our favorite verses, and give them away. Or we can leave encouraging sticky-note messages in visible, public places like restroom mirrors.

If you really want to get creative and have some fun with words, make a flyer with tear-off tabs for a community bulletin board. You know the ones that typically have phone numbers hanging off the bottom? Except rather than advertising something and leaving a contact number, simply say, "Take what you need." The front of the tabs could then say: *Love, Hope, Faith, Encouragement, Peace,* and *Patience.* The other side would share an uplifting quote or Bible verse of your choosing. Sounds like a rewarding project for a youth group or scout troop.

If you would like to replicate this idea, here are some great Bible verses to help you get started. Or, you can just take what *you* need today!

Love—Psalm 118:1 NIV
Give thanks to the LORD for he is good; his love endures forever.

Hope—Jeremiah 29:11 NIV
"I know the plans I have for you," declares the LORD, "plans to prosper you and not to harm you, plans to give you hope and a future."

Perspective—Matthew 6:34
Don't worry about tomorrow, for tomorrow will bring its own worries. Today's trouble is enough for today.

Comfort—Isaiah 41:10 NIV
Do not fear, for I am with you; do not be dismayed, for I am your God. I will strengthen you and help you; I will uphold you with my righteous right hand.

Courage—Philippians 4:13 NKJV
I can do all things through Christ who strengthens me.

Peace—John 14:27
I am leaving you with a gift—peace of mind and heart. And the peace I give is a gift the world cannot give. So don't be troubled or afraid.

Guidance—Proverbs 3:5
Trust in the LORD with all your heart; do not depend on your own understanding. Seek his will in all you do, and he will show you which path to take.

Faith—Romans 8:28 NIV
We know that in all things God works for the good of those who love him, who have been called according to his purpose.

Perseverance—James 1:2–3 NIV
Consider it pure joy, my brothers and sisters, whenever you face trials of many kinds, because you know that the testing of your faith produces perseverance.

Confidence—Psalm 139:14 NKJV
I will praise You, for I am fearfully and wonderfully made; marvelous are Your works, and that my soul knows very well.

We face challenges every day, but challenges can be softened by an atmosphere of encouragement. The messages surrounding us have the power to lift us up, push us forward, and cheer us on. Written or spoken, we can create echoes of goodness with our words, using them to change hearts and enrich lives.

Gracious words are a honeycomb,
sweet to the soul and healing to the bones.
PROVERBS 16:24 NIV

CHAPTER 23

PAY DAY

SEVERAL YEARS BEFORE I embarked on my kindness journey, I was the recipient of a random act of kindness. My daughter and I were in line at our favorite sandwich shop, when the man in front of us looked our way with a genuine smile. "I'd like to pay for their meals too, please," he told the cashier. My preschooler looked at him with her big blue eyes and queried, "Why would you do that?" Swallowing a laugh, he shared that he does an act of kindness every Friday. He simply wanted to treat us to lunch. TGIF! We accepted his generosity, including the cookie he added for my daughter, and left the restaurant with our hearts as full as our bellies.

The cost of his act of kindness was about ten dollars. The time it took was approximately five minutes. The impact . . . infinite. He lit up the face of a child and inspired a great conversation on the ride home. He clearly touched my life; I even wrote about our "unexpected perk kind of a day" in an old journal. I remember the people around us had smiles on their faces. And I can only imagine how his simple gesture impacted the woman working at the shop.

A remarkable thing about kindness is that we never know where it will end up. (There's that ripple again.) It's fascinating to speculate what one person can accomplish with only one act of kindness each week. Directly and indirectly, thousands of lives could be impacted—a good reason for continuing kindness beyond our forty days!

If one person could impact thousands of lives, what would happen if masses of people were spreading kindness regularly? We might just start to see a shift from *selfies* to *selflessness*. Perhaps our faith in humanity would slowly be restored as generosity and goodness became the norm.

We learn what we see, so if we see more people choosing love, we will expect love. That will result in even more goodness. In this scenario, it would no longer be shocking to be blessed by kindness for no reason. We can work together to create a world where the ugly behavior is the unexpected, surprising choice.

As we think about the effects of committing to kindness, the opportunities are abundant. And while many ideas do not involve financial commitment, there are many ways to open hearts by opening our wallets.

A bighearted businessman in my hometown community set a great example for committing to kindness. Mr. D. lived his life in a ready position, eager to help others every chance he got. His daughter once said, "He knew every gift he had was from God, and he just wanted to share it." One simple kindness he did on a regular basis delivered endless smiles. Whenever he walked into a high school sporting event, his first order of business was to go directly to the concession stand. He'd buy about forty Blow Pops and stuff them in every pocket and crevice of his suit jacket. As he walked to his seat, he would pass them out to the kids he passed. Small cost. Big fun.

The possibilities for acts of kindness with a dollar sign continue. We can triple the tip. Order dessert for another table at a restaurant and have it delivered after we leave. Keep $5 gift cards on hand, sharing them anonymously as inspired. We can pay for the person behind us at a toll booth, a pay-first parking lot, or a drive-thru window. When returning a Redbox movie, treat the next person by slipping two dollars inside the DVD case. Pay for someone's overdue library bill or a lay-away order. Lighten the financial burden of a friend or family member. Create a "coins for a cause" jar, collecting household loose change for a different charity each month. Stash a dollar on a shelf in the dollar store. Leave a scratch-off lottery ticket under the windshield wiper of someone's car. (What a relief to realize it isn't a parking ticket!)

Kindness card alert! All these ideas involving money are perfect opportunities to use a kindness card. The person working the drive-thru window will happily give a card along with the fun news that the car driving away took care of the bill.

That little card packs a giant message of hope. Sadly, in a world where kindness is not quite the norm, a world where we witness more and more despair, receiving a reminder of prevailing goodness can get someone through a tough day. And that, sweet friends, is the ultimate answer to my daughter's question, "Why would you do that?"

We do that because it makes someone happy. We do that because it can inspire others. We do that because it fills us up. We do that because we are called to love.

For where your treasure is, there your heart will also be.

MATTHEW 6:21 NIV

CHAPTER 24

SHARE A PRAYER

IT WAS ONE OF THOSE DAYS. Running on empty, wishing for more hours in the week. I was genuinely thankful to serve God with my taps on the keyboard, yet my confidence was teetering like the glass I'd knocked over at breakfast. Frazzled. Fragile.

I walked out to the mailbox for some air and there, tucked between boring bills, junk mail, and catalogs, was a small hand-written card from my high school alma mater, St. John in Ashtabula, Ohio—the Fighting Heralds. Eager for a taste of home, I tore open the envelope to find an endearing treasure. "Today we have prayed for you by name." Instant smile. I continued reading, moved by the letter's beautiful words about the power and purpose of prayer. And in the middle of the page was a message I desperately needed in that moment: "We have asked God to inspire you with whatever gift you most need today."

Isn't it awesome when God shows up right on cue? When He uses our brothers and sisters to give us precisely what we need. When He reminds us that we are not alone.

I thought about the students at the school, the girls wearing the identical plaid skirt and knee-high socks that I'd rocked twenty-five years ago (along with big ole permed hair doused in Aqua Net). And while their world is vastly different—cell phones, laptops, Smart Boards, iPads, Instagram, YouTube, and everything in between—the best connection for reaching across the miles and across all boundaries, is still exactly the same: prayer.

Hopeful that the students realized their impact on alumni through prayer, I was moved by the image of another generation of Heralds doing the same for them one day. Covering them in prayer. By name. And the timeless touch of this sacred connection continues. Without end.

While prayer is our direct line to the Lord, it is also a powerful way to communicate with one another. Over the years, I've discovered that the best way to pour into others through prayer is by committing to our own prayer life. The more we prioritize prayer and the more continual it becomes in our day, then the more acutely we experience God's presence, and the more comfortable we feel praying for and with others.

When we engage in prayer for another person, we are presenting them to God and drawing them close to our hearts. We are also strengthening our relationship with Jesus in the process.

But why bother? Why should we pray for others?

Because it works.

We don't always get the answers we want, but prayer always

impacts *something*. Prayer can offer peace, change a heart, reveal an opportunity, provide perspective, or build a relationship. It might even move a mountain! Each time we pray, God works in our lives.

In Max Lucado's book *Before Amen*, he says, "You are never more like Jesus than when you pray for others. Pray for those you love; pray for those you don't. Pray for this hurting world."

Talk about an opportunity to love others wherever we are! We can close our eyes right now and pray for someone in our lives, even send a quick text to let them know we're keeping them close in prayer. Just like the joy I received from my high school, knowing that we've been prayed for is comforting. It embraces us with the promise of support; it reminds us to pray.

Quietly. Aloud. Together. Alone. Spoken. Written. Moments. Hours. There is no right way and no limit to how we can reach others through prayer. We can send a praise song we think a friend would enjoy. Start a prayer group in our community. Ask if we can pray with someone when they share a struggle. Write a Bible verse on a small rock and give it to a friend as a prayer tool. Teach kids to pray. Send a prayer shawl or prayer pillow. We can pray on the spot—pray when we hear an ambulance or fire truck, pray for countries without clean water when we effortlessly grab a drink from the tap, pray for military families when we pass someone in uniform, pray for the hungry when we walk through the grocery store, pray for school communities when we see a school bus, pray for our leadership when we see stars and stripes. Pray.

An enthusiastic woman shared her experiences of doing Forty Days of Kindness with her church. She recognized that consecutive kindness could move her away from being self-absorbed, something she'd always struggled with. Committed to improving herself and helping others, she sought out to pray intently every day. In addition to her prayers, she intentionally reached out to the people she prayed for. She would send a note, give a call, or share in person that she prayed for them that week. During this process, she found that more people began asking her for prayer because they were confident that she would do it. And . . . she made huge strides in shifting her focus from self to others.

Praying for others helps us to think outside of our own needs. It provides unity, hope, and healing. We are reminded, through the power of prayer, that we are not alone in our inevitable struggles. We have a loving God. And we have one another.

The earnest prayer of a righteous person has great power
and produces wonderful results.

JAMES 5:16

CHAPTER 25

WARM WELCOME

I WAS IN THE ZONE on my morning walk. Headphones blasting Zumba masterpieces, I bounced along, celebrating a return to some much needed structure at summer's end. A school bus zoomed by, startling me from my trance. My attention was drawn to my neighbor's front yard. A large sign was staked in the grass, and several attached balloons danced in the wind.

With a closer look, I realized it was a welcome sign. The kids were starting at a new school, and the simple yard decoration screamed, "Can't wait to meet you—we're so glad you're joining us!"

Wow! This gesture made an impact on *me,* and I was just passing by. I can't imagine the joy on the children's faces. A burst of sunshine during an uncertain transition.

We've all been there. The stranger in the crowd. The new addition. The one standing outside the circle. And I bet we remember the person who opened that circle and made room for one more.

I had the incredible privilege of spending my entire junior year of college in Italy. The home of my ancestors, the birthplace of my mom . . . I could not have been more excited to connect with the culture. Throughout my childhood, all five senses had been fully engaged in Italian everything, shared with great love by my amazing grandparents. I spent hours looking at pictures of our cherished homeland. Smelling fresh parsley from Papa Guy's impressive garden. Eating, eating, and more eating in Noni's well-loved kitchen. Dancing the tarantella with my adored cousins. Hearing stories of the war and my family's journey to America through tears of nostalgia for a life left behind.

I was awed at the mere thought of getting to reverse the journey and head back to where it all began. And I naively assumed I would fit right in, since I am, after all, Italian.

I realized a few things very quickly upon arrival in Rome. My Italian speaking skills might have allowed me to communicate with a toddler. I could be spotted from about a mile away as an American in a foreign land. And my new city was stunning (eventually winning a huge piece of my heart), but intensely over-stimulating and filled with almost three million people! A far cry from my small town, where I learned all about Italy in the comfort of my grandparents' loving home.

I wasn't in Kansas anymore, Toto. And I was wondering if a click of my heels could send me back to something familiar.

When I arrived at my residence, Villa Nazareth, I was greeted by a sign on my door that said *Benvenuto!* And the twelve Italian girls who would be my housemates for the next year were there to greet me with open arms. None of them spoke English, but they all spoke the universal language of kindness, and they spoke it fluently.

Before I even had my bag unpacked, my roommate, Carmen, handed me a helmet and pointed to her Vespa. We zipped around the narrow streets of Rome for hours, and she continued to be my personal tour guide for the next couple of weeks as I got situated. Showing me the sights. Instructing me on how to navigate public transportation. Taking me to the bank and the embassy to handle boring paperwork—all things that would have been an enormous challenge without her help.

My compassionate housemates continued to shower me with affection throughout my year abroad. Many of them even invited me to their homes in other regions of Italy for holidays and special celebrations. Their immediate willingness and effort to welcome an outsider made all the difference for my experience and fostered lasting friendships. I was able to fully enjoy my adventure and explore my roots because of their support.

There is a sacredness to the act of drawing people in, of changing their status from stranger to friend. Jesus was the perfect model of reaching others through a warm welcome. He sought out the newcomer, the outcast, even when they were shunned by the masses (Luke 15:1–2). He practiced hospitality in the most holy sense of the word.

The mere thought of *hospitality* can make some of us perspire. We have a Pinterest panic attack and feel immediately inadequate, not capable of living up to the expectations of Martha Stewart. But hospitality doesn't need to be complex or accented with a burlap bow; hospitality is simply loving others, making them feel comfortable and valued. In fact, the Greek word for hospitality, *xenia*, is defined as "the generosity and courtesy shown to those who are far from home."

Whether a person is "far from home" in a literal sense or just feeling the loss of a cozy comfort zone, we can offer a hand to hold and a steady ground on which to gain momentum.

We can reach out to new neighbors with a visit, a dinner invite, a welcome party, or a delivery of baked goods or local produce. Be aware—learn to recognize and respond when someone looks lost or disconnected. Go out of the way to meet the visitors at church. Make a list of resources to share with people new to the community—preschools, moms' clubs, doctors, churches, grocery stores, hiking trails, contractors, recreation programs, parks, libraries, and restaurants.

We can teach our kids about the importance of including new classmates and teammates, and the great opportunity to make a new friend. Smile. Ask questions—try "What do you do for fun?" rather than "what do you do?" Scooch over and make room. Open our homes and our hearts. Introduce ourselves . . . introduce others. Then, after some time passes, we can call to check in or meet for lunch at a favorite local hot spot.

Welcome. It's such a happy word, creating an instant sense of comfort and belonging. When we accept the challenge to open our circle and invite someone in, we have the privilege of turning reluctance into relief, intimidation into inclusion, fear into friendship. We can make a gigantic impact with a teeny tiny gesture of love. It's serving others while serving Christ.

Don't forget to show hospitality to strangers,
for some who have done this have
entertained angels without realizing it!
HEBREWS 13:2–3

CHAPTER 26

LEAN IN AND LISTEN

I STOOD AT THE BULLETIN BOARD in our church gathering area, soaking in the good deeds that had been shared during our Forty Days of Kindness ministry. Along with a sign-up sheet, inspirational quotes, and a list of practical kindness ideas, the board was covered in heart-shaped sticky notes.

The notes were a refreshing, old-school way for people to post their insights and experiences.

Wrote a "love letter" to a teen struggling with self-esteem.

For all forty days, I'm letting everyone who needs to merge into my lane go in front of me.

Held a door open for ten consecutive people.

Left a cookie and a kindness card for our waitress.

Helped change a tire.

While I was admiring the display, a woman walked up and thoughtfully wrote three words on a paper heart. "Learning to Listen."

Interested, I asked if she would mind telling me about her kindness journey. The bright-eyed woman graciously revealed that she struggles with listening. She gets distracted. She zones out. She thinks about other things. She mentally reviews the day's schedule. She ponders what to say next. Her kindness adventure had become a quest for more attentive ears. She continually sought to be a more engaged listener, and she was seeing results! Each conversation left her increasingly convinced that listening is the greatest tool God gave us for helping people.

With a wandering brain of my own, I was intrigued to connect the dots between focused listening and kindness. When we aren't fully present in our interactions, we may miss an opportunity to show love. For example, if a friend tells us they are starting a new job on a certain date, by listening intently we can remember the date or write it in our calendar, and send a card or a quick "thinking of you" text on the big day.

Each word that misses our ears carries the possibility of a deeper connection, an answered prayer, a need fulfilled. We can't offer help or reach out with gestures of kindness if we aren't listening. Our attentiveness directly affects our actions.

Ironically, the action people frequently seek *is* listening.

Do you ever back away from an intense conversation or urgently try to fix another person's situation by offering advice, interrupting, or relating a story from your life? I'm afraid I have. But often what the other person really desires is just a listening ear. Someone to show concern. Someone to patiently hear their story. Someone to ask, "How are you?" and welcome the real answer.

Talking helps us hear our own thoughts and discover our own solutions; the trick is having someone who will listen. Really listen. Uncrossed arms, phone out of sight, oblivious to time, looking into our eyes, leaning in for a good long listen.

One of the most rewarding experiences I have had came through a volunteer position at a local children's hospital. I was a part of the pastoral care team, and my role was to offer spiritual and emotional support to families in the hospital. I was assigned to a different unit each time I volunteered, and I would make my rounds, visiting the kids and their family members.

When I first began this work, I was mildly terrified. There was a passion inside of me to be there, but I really couldn't imagine what I would say to provide comfort to the families who were literally fighting for their children's lives. I would pray for the right words, the perfect prayer, something insightful to bring peace. And what I found out very quickly was that my ears were in much greater demand than my mouth.

With this acute appreciation and commitment to listening, I

walked into a room one morning in the Neonatal Intensive Care Unit. I sat and visited with a mom for a while, and during our conversation she said one short, subtle sentence that jumped out at me like a jack-in-the-box. Her words implied self-blame, guilt over her baby's illness. She was caught in a perpetual examination of her pregnancy, certain she had somehow caused this difficult situation.

One sentence.

If I had zoned out, quickly checked my phone, or thought for a few seconds about what I wanted for lunch, I would have missed it.

I honestly didn't do anything skillful or exceptional after I heard her words of assumed responsibility. I just acknowledged that she said it. And that was all it took for her to release the five-ton weight she had been carrying around. She emoted and poured it all out, which was a good start to finding some peace. And I listened.

Since I moved from unit to unit, I didn't see her after that day. About a month later, I found a card in the pastoral care office with my name on it. She shared that she was finally able to take her baby home, and she thanked me for the time I had spent with her on that one visit. Admitting her fear aloud had begun a healing process for her. She had even worked up the courage to talk with her baby's doctors about her concerns, which led to more peace of mind.

In big moments and in our everyday conversations with others, we can offer a beaming source of light just by being attentive and providing a trusted sounding board. And what an honor it is to get to enter another person's story, into their world. A sacred privilege.

But how do we go about enhancing the work of our ears?

Demonstrated by the woman at the bulletin board and my own growth in this area, listening is a decision. It takes practice, an awareness of how much we speak versus how much we listen, a commitment to staying engaged in our conversations, and a deliberate pulling ourselves back if our mind wanders over to the grocery list.

Reading through any of the four Gospels in the Bible, we will see Jesus repeatedly showing solid listening skills. He stops to talk with people. He never rushes. He's respectful. He shows genuine interest and concern. He asks questions. He seeks to understand. He puts aside His own agenda. He draws people in. He responds with loving action.

If we reflect on how *we* feel when we are truly heard, we'll quickly recognize the value of intentional listening. Leaning in to listen creates a window to the face of Jesus, reminding others of His boundless love through our presence, our compassion.

My dear brothers and sisters:
You must all be quick to listen, slow to speak,
and slow to get angry.
JAMES 1:19

CHAPTER 27

TOGETHER WE WILL SERVE

COMMUNITY SERVICE SATURDAY—the grand finale for Forty Days of Kindness at my home church. During the second year of our kindness initiative, our pastors added an incredible community outreach which has now become an annual event. Families quickly fill in the sign-up sheets, excited for an organized way to serve together. We take to the streets with smiling faces and bright yellow shirts proudly proclaiming, "God's Work, Our Hands." And the best part is, the hands come in all sizes. There is something for everyone; even the youngest among us can serve.

During the first Community Service Saturday, my family played bingo at a nursing home as our act of service. Our kids were six, nine, and eleven, and they were all able to engage in this rewarding outreach. Eventually. When we first arrived, they were hesitant. They stood quietly off to the side, unsure of what to do and how to interact with a population they had spent very little time with.

After some time to warm up, our six-year-old was calling out the letters and numbers for the game. He was quickly told that he needed to "talk a whole lot louder than that, young fella." Loud and clear, he yelled out "N–21." One of the residents cheered for him, and he looked at me with a triumphant grin.

My older son found a seat next to a resident wearing an Ohio State Buckeyes hat. They became fast friends as they worked together toward a bingo. And my daughter joyfully pulled around a little red wagon to all the winners, helping them select the perfect prize. Snacks were the biggest hit for the men; the women were all about the costume jewelry!

Everyone had a good time. We got to know the sweet family from our church that we'd randomly been assigned to serve with. The kids stepped out of their comfort zone, expanding their view on how to make a difference in the world and continuing to grow with each opportunity to love others on purpose.

While we were at the nursing home, other families from our church were off spreading kindness in other ways throughout our county. Beautifying a homeless shelter. Gleaning crops for a food bank. Helping with repairs at the domestic violence center. Organizing donations. Gardening at a drug and alcohol treatment house. Assembling dinners to freeze and distribute. Preparing nonperishable breakfast bags for shut-ins. Painting housing units. Decorating cards and notes of encouragement.

It was a joyful day.

Whether we're participating in a ready-to-go project or crafting our own outreach initiative, the benefits of walking in service beside children and teens extend far beyond the work of our hands. The real work happens in the heart—ours and theirs. We model Christian values in action. We create positive energy. We bring our families closer together. We strengthen communities. We build life skills and self-esteem. We cultivate a genuine respect and desire for giving back. We provide a broadened perspective.

Serving with the children in our lives sets them on a victorious path, a path we can be proud to pave for them. Through the work of their hands and the goodness in their souls, they are not only nurturing themselves and others, but serving Christ as well. In Matthew 25:35–36, Jesus shares a parable, proclaiming: "For I was hungry, and you fed me. I was thirsty, and you gave me a drink. I was a stranger, and you invited me into your home. I was naked, and you gave me clothing. I was sick, and you cared for me. I was in prison, and you visited me." When the people questioned Jesus, asking when they had ministered to Him in those ways, He responded, "I tell you the truth, when you did it to one of the least of these my brothers and sisters, you were doing it to me" (Matthew 25:40).

With much to give and much to gain, the prospect of family service projects is exciting. But I often find that my calendar is so filled with other obligations that I struggle to get beyond interest and intention. Anyone with me? I sincerely desire to do more outreach with my children and other groups of kids in my life, to connect more deeply by serving together. I want to help prepare the next generation to lead in love and to focus on selflessness. And yet I allow other activities to take the lead. Repeatedly.

So, what next? For those of us who are inconsistent with follow through, how do we get from consideration to commitment?

A good way to begin is by finding a local need. Our communities are brimming with opportunities for helping others. Churches should have a pulse on where we can lend a hand; we can also get great ideas by talking with friends and neighbors. Another exceptional resource is the United Way, unitedway.org. The website's tool, "Find Your United Way," will lead users to their local chapters. Many local United Way sites have links to partner agencies and local volunteer opportunities. Also, websites like serve.gov; volunteermatch.org; pointsoflight.org; and createthegood.org will match interests and location with volunteer opportunities. You may be surprised at what is happening right in your town.

Once we have a handle on the available volunteering options, we can start narrowing down what works best for our family or group, including having a conversation with the kids about their interests. I've found that creating consistency is an effective strategy. Make regular room for community service; find agencies with recurring activities and schedule them into the family's monthly calendar. Team up with another family for accountability and fellowship.

What a privilege it is to shape and direct young lives. I'm ready to clear out some time and shift my focus, reminding myself and my children that we are servants of Jesus, not servants of our schedules.

Direct your children onto the right path,
and when they are older, they will not leave it.
PROVERBS 22:6

CHAPTER 28

TRADITION MISSION

IN 2007, TRICIA, a woman with a servant's heart, began something she humbly refers to as a "little Thanksgiving project." The official name of the outreach has become Feast for Families, and it continues to bless countless lives. The first year of the project, Tricia enlisted thirty ladies in her community to spread love during the holidays. These women united to feed local families and to teach their own children the joy in giving.

The first year, nine families received homemade Thanksgiving feasts. As the years progressed, more peopled wanted to get involved, and more families in need were served. A simple formula for the project was determined (replicate away!)

For every team of six adult volunteers, three families can be fed. (The families range from four to six people). Each volunteer provides fifteen dollars and one side dish for their three families: green bean casserole, mashed potatoes, pumpkin pie, sweet potatoes, stuffing or rolls, butter, and gravy. The money is used to purchase turkeys, turkey pans, turkey bags, broth, and whipped cream. The recipient families cook the turkey themselves with detailed directions.

Easy concept. Enormous impact. Fast forward nine years. One community. Two hundred eighty-nine adults prepared food. Four hundred exhilarated kids assembled the donations. One hundred forty-eight families were fed. Countless lives were touched.

Shortly after Thanksgiving, Tricia received a touching thank-you note from one of the families they'd served. A struggling mom shared that only God knew how heartbroken she had been because she could not provide Thanksgiving dinner for her family. New to the area, she was certain the Holy Spirit had led her to Feast for Families. She thanked Tricia for showing her that God still speaks to people to do His work.

The mom went on to write that the image of a family standing at her door with love and a beautiful, bountiful box of food is something she will never forget. After the delivery, she and her family stood looking at the feast before them. Then her five-year-old son, Jacob, said "I don't know if those were real people or angels sent from God." Jacob's older brother replied, "Oh, those were human angels."

Across the state, during the same period of time, another family was busy with an annual holiday project too. It all started when a little girl named Maren befriended a new classmate, Chloe.

Chloe had an endearing spirit, but sadness in her eyes. She had recently been plucked from her school and her friends, because her mom had started a drug and alcohol rehab program. The rehab center was unique in that children could stay with their moms for the duration of treatment. It was a wonderful gift but a tough transition for Chloe.

Maren's compassion and affection toward Chloe grew, and she asked her parents if there was something they could do to help. With a phone call to the treatment residence, Maren's family learned of an urgent need for the upcoming holidays. They were seeking filled stockings to give the moms and children on Christmas morning. Maren's family drafted an e-mail to ask for help, and their friends came through with nearly fifty beautiful, overflowing stockings topped with love, hope, and generosity. This outreach, lovingly named Jingle Stockings, became an annual December ministry, blessing the families on both the giving and the receiving ends of the project.

In addition to providing stockings each year, Maren's connection to the treatment facility trickled over to their church family, creating a valuable and enduring relationship. The partnership with the treatment center now offers ongoing service opportunities for the church's youth programs and community outreach. And the recovering families are continually blessed by loving hands.

We never know how outreach traditions will begin, but they have a unique way of creating a profound effect. Every year brings opportunities for more growth, more reach. We're able to draw new people in and refine the project along the way.

If we keep our eyes open for kindness traditions in our

community (they are plentiful in November and December), we may stumble upon something we'll look forward to each year. If you'd like to ignite something, even just within your own family, looking at the calendar can spark some ideas.

We can organize a school supply collection every August for local kids in need. Bring a ton of popsicles to a busy park on the first day of summer. Bake cookies on Veterans Day and take them to the VA hospital. Make an acts-of-kindness advent calendar. Show love to a local hospital on Valentine's Day or make "busy bags" for the ER waiting room by decorating plain white gift bags and filling them with coloring books, crayons, card games, books, and snacks. Do a good deed to celebrate the birthday of someone who has passed. Plan an Easter egg hunt or a Fourth of July bike parade for your neighborhood. Plan a "cheer tree" making party where kids of any age decorate a small, peppy Christmas tree (wooden ornaments colored with markers work best) and deliver it to a special place in the community during the holidays—hospitals, nursing homes, cancer centers, or homeless shelters. Make donut deliveries on the first Friday of June, National Donut Day.

Traditions built on love can also center on our own friends and family. My husband's Grandpa Arnold made a delicious delicacy every year for the Christmas season—chocolate toffee sprinkled with joy. He shared that special Christmas candy, and we enjoyed it at every opportunity. It often appeared on the fellowship table at church; he even mailed it to long-distance loved ones. When Arnold passed away, he had been making the candy for sixty years! His grandson Doug has now taken over the tradition, and he handles it with just as much love and dedication.

Tradition! Complicated or simple, massive or intimate—kindness traditions keep the goodness flowing. They provide built-in occasions each year to spread love and inspire others to join us!

---

*Think of ways to motivate one another
to acts of love and good works.*
HEBREWS 10:24

CHAPTER 29

OPERATION IMITATION

WHICH ONE OF THESE was not like the other? Yep, it was me. I was the only person at the dinner party holding a baby. My husband and I were in a parenting stage that required toting the infant or missing the event. The moment I entered the magnificent house, I was fairly certain we had made the wrong choice. Too late to turn around and go home? Afraid so.

After some hugs, handshakes, and warm welcomes to our miniature partygoer, I started to loosen up. The sea of new faces smiled in acceptance of our predicament, clearly happy we were there.

As we sat down for dinner, the fussy little one still in my arms, the hostess of the party took me by enormous surprise. She approached me and quietly asked if I would please allow her to take the baby so I could eat in peace. Glancing up at the photos of her school-aged children, she shared that she remembered the challenges of those exhausting newborn days, and she was certain I could use a break. She was right.

Gently persistent, this generous new friend left the room with my bundle of tears, assuring me she could handle it. She was right again.

The impression of this selfless offering surpassed even the bliss of a delicious meal enjoyed in unusual tranquility. Even today, I smile as I remember her compassion.

During my preparation for Forty Days of Kindness, one of the strategies I used for generating a game plan was reflection. I spent time reflecting on my role as a receiver of everyday gestures of kindness, calling to mind simple good deeds that left an enduring impact.

I remembered the professor who had given me a picture from his office wall because I complimented its beauty. The housekeeping staff member at a hotel who mailed my daughter her beloved, missing blanket when it turned up months after we called about it. An acquaintance who voluntarily spent an afternoon tutoring me when we brought home our Boston terrier, Yoda—my first dog . . . I was clueless. A thoroughly planned surprise visit from my brother, when his humor and support were just what I needed. A couple who discretely picked up the dinner bill for our whole group of fancy high school friends heading off to a homecoming dance. A friend who planted cheerful spring bulbs in my yard without my knowledge—the gift that keeps on giving!

And there is one gesture I love to replicate whenever given the chance. During my daughter's Girl Scout days, seven girls from our troop were manning a cookie booth inside a hardware store. Business was slow, and we'd even had some rude interactions that left me feeling disappointed in humanity.

Just as we were ready to throw in the towel for the day and close up shop, a man walked up to the booth. Through a full gray beard, he said to the girls: "I already bought cookies from my niece, but I'd like to buy a box for each of you." He paid for seven boxes of cookies and told each of the girls to pick their favorite kind and take it home to their family. The kids were jubilant and incredibly grateful. But even more than a box of cookies, they all received a necessary reminder of goodness. And they all left their post with a great example of showing kindness while going about a typical day.

The common denominator for these gestures is their purity. There were no traces of obligation—the motive was sincere, intentional kindness.

What comes to mind when you reflect on receiving acts of love? Connecting with memories is a great way to get fired up about spreading kindness; it's also a foolproof action plan. Think of a good deed done for you, a realistic gesture that left a glowing imprint, and pay it forward!

If you're celebrating Forty Days of Kindness with your family or a small group of people, this reflection exercise is fun to do together. It's collaborative, uplifting, and infectious. You could even start a "caught-in-the-act" notebook or poster, a place to document acts of kindness received or witnessed.

Paying attention to the positive energy around us keeps us invigorated and inspired. When our eyes are scanning for kindness, we'll quickly discover that we are surrounded by people worthy of imitation!

Follow my example,
as I follow the example of Christ.
1 Corinthians 11:1 niv

CHAPTER 30

AROUND THE WORLD

OVERHEARING THE TENDER conversation in the other room among our children, my friend and I suddenly went quiet. The kids had seen a photograph of a World Vision child on the refrigerator, and they were comparing notes about their sponsored children! *How old is he? What's her name? Which country is he from? Do you send e-mails?*

My friend shared that she had walked past the sponsorship cards at the Christian bookstore countless times, but it wasn't until her family participated in Forty Days of Kindness at our church that they decided to sponsor a child. It was a decision, she said, that enriched their lives far beyond their expectations. Getting to know their sponsored child and learning about her community made them all more aware, more compassionate, more appreciative.

Child sponsorship has blessed my family in the same way, helping both the kids and the adults remember that there is a big world out there that looks quite different than the one we experience every day. The kids have watched videos of our child and her community. And while they know that she lives in a bamboo house with dirt floors, they also know that she loves soccer and she colors a picture like a champ! They feel connected to her through their e-mail and letter exchanges, the uplifting reviews of how our support has helped her and her community, and the prayers we send her way continually.

As my friend and I chatted about our mutual experience, we realized that the mediocre pizzas we had bought for lunch that afternoon cost more than our monthly payment to sponsor a child! Our commitment was going further than we could imagine, unquestionably providing vital resources like food, healthcare, education, economic development, clean water, and God's Word to our sponsored kids and their communities. We also can make special contributions for very specific needs for our sponsored family and even help the kids in the community to have birthday celebrations.

These impoverished communities are part of a startling statistic on the World Vision website stating that, "More than seven hundred million people worldwide are living on less than $1.90 a day." *One dollar and ninety cents a day.* That's less than the cost of a sixteen-ounce coffee at Starbucks.

Looking at global giving through this lens illuminates the impact we can make from wherever we are, with whatever we have. As we discover ways to personally connect on an international level, the world starts to feel smaller and more intimate. Our eyes open to possibilities like celebrating a loved one's birthday globally by giving a goat, chickens, or a fishing kit in their honor rather than a gift that adds to excess (heifer.org).

And with every gesture, we begin to recognize that we *can* help. We can help fight poverty. We can help provide clean water. We can help with disaster relief. We can help the sick. We can help women and children who are mistreated. We can help countries devastated by war. We can help empower struggling communities. We can help deliver the liberating message of Jesus. We *can* help.

Particularly now, with advancements in technology, we have more access than ever to educate ourselves and get involved on a global scale. A great place to witness an extensive reach is on the World Vision website, worldvision.org. Also, if you're considering the ministry of child sponsorship, you can see photos, learn about the children, and even finalize sponsorship online.

World Vision is not alone. Organizations that transform lives around the globe are diverse and vast. One such organization, Convoy of Hope (convoyofhope.org), has helped over 79 million people through their passionate commitment to feeding the world. Ladies, search *Party 2 Empower* on the Convoy of Hope website to find out how to host a party for a cause. It's a great way to get together with friends while supporting an initiative that empowers women. In one year, this non-profit helped 640 women start businesses so they can sustain their families.

We can also find a wealth of information from our local churches regarding global partnerships; local churches make enormous strides for worldwide issues.

A nondenominational church in my area has a different global ministry for each Sunday school level; their kindergarten and first graders have raised enough money to free seventeen slaves through the International Justice Mission (IJM.org). IJM is a global team of lawyers, investigators, social workers, and community activists who serve to rescue and restore victims of violence in developing countries.

The kids at this church are passionate about helping to bring people to freedom. A children's ministry staff member at the church shared that kids at every age continue to help with this outreach. The high school youth group sought to raise funds for IJM one Sunday by washing car windows and tires while church members were in their worship service. The students had placed collection envelopes in the church bulletin the week before, and whoever wanted their cars cleaned for a great cause simply stuck the envelope with their donation under their windshield wiper. Clever! The teens did this for all three church services on both of their church campuses, and the group raised $4,000 in one day! An amazing testimony to introducing children to their capacity to help others from a young age.

At my home church, also with our youth taking the lead, we collected enough funds to donate three water wells within rural Africa through a nonprofit organization called Water to Thrive (watertothrive.org). It's difficult to fully understand the impact of the water crisis in our world. Nearly a billion people worldwide do not have access to clean, safe water. Through some friendly competition started by a rock-star Sunday school teacher, the kids in our church were excited to earn their own money and contribute to this worthwhile, lifesaving cause.

If you'd like to learn more about global programs within our reach, the national websites of Christian denominations have links to their global missions, offering exceptional resources for ministry opportunities. These few sites are a great starting point for discovering opportunities, ranging from monetary donations all the way to mission work:

Catholic Relief Services: crs.org
Episcopal Church: episcopalchurch.org
Evangelical Lutheran Church of America: elca.org
Presbyterian Church of America: pcanet.org
Southern Baptist Conference: sbc.net
United Methodist Church: umc.org

Equipping ourselves with ways to bring peace to a hurting world is empowering. With Jesus as our model, we can turn compassion into action (Mark 8:1–10). No matter the size, our gestures of generosity have no walls. Kindness will cross oceans, climb mountains, and transform lives.

Give, and it will be given to you. A good measure, pressed down, shaken together and running over, will be poured into your lap. For with the measure you use, it will be measured to you.
Luke 6:38 niv

CHAPTER 31

LIFE-GIVING BODIES

SHE STOOD IN FRONT of the congregation, and all eyes were on her, many of them filled with tears. With confidence and ease, the courageous twenty-four-year-old woman, Jacky, spoke from the heart. She shared her transformational story: a decision that had changed her forever, saved her best friend's life, and awed the people witnessing their journey.

With a conviction she credited fully to God, she simplified her experience to one sentence, "Well, my friend Jillian needed a kidney, and so I gave her one of mine."

She had our attention.

Her story rained God's blessings on all of us. It was impossible to miss His presence and His careful planning. A last-minute roommate switch in college had placed these two strangers together. They experienced an instant connection and an unusually perfect match for the transplant . . . just in time. The story continued with three successful twenty-one-vial blood draws from a kid who *always* fainted during the needle-blood combo. Overwhelming reassurance at every turn. Unwavering certainty that, beyond the limit of words, God was working through her. And . . . *and*! Jillian's family received the gift of faith through this experience. Amen.

It's amazing to think about the intricacies of our physical bodies and the needs that arise when we least expect them and the opportunities available to help others—to even save a life—in ways we haven't considered.

From the very top of our heads, there are opportunities to impact others with blessings from our bodies. A simple and exciting possibility is through donation of our hair. Locks of Love is a nonprofit organization that offers hairpieces for children with financial need in the United States and Canada, an exciting way for kids to serve other kids. Detailed information is available on LocksOfLove. org. Pantene Beautiful Lengths has a similar program for women battling cancer. Take a look at pantene.com.

We can significantly bless others by giving blood. Did you know that every two seconds someone in the United States needs blood? Information on blood and platelet donation is available at RedCrossBlood.org. We may even choose to involve our work, church, or other organizations by hosting a blood drive.

While blood drives and blood donations are outreaches we often hear about, bone marrow is another type of donation that is in urgent need around the world.

A few years ago, my friend Amanda casually asked if I could watch her son one morning before school because she had to be at the hospital super early. When I nosily inquired about why she was going to the hospital, she told me that she was donating her bone marrow. To a stranger. When I pried further into her personal business, she shared an incredible story.

Twenty years earlier, a friend of her husband was diagnosed with leukemia and needed a bone marrow transplant. Friends and family attended a bone marrow registry drive, desperately seeking a match to save their friend. (The initial process at the time involved a blood draw, but today it is a simple cheek swab.) Amanda was not a match that day. But she chose to stay in the registry, in case she could ever help someone else battling blood cancer.

Two decades later, a young woman across the ocean was fighting for her life. And Amanda had the bone marrow that could save her. She was the match!

I marveled at her plans for the day and commented on how incredibly fortunate and full of hope the woman suffering from cancer must feel, knowing someone was able and willing to help her. Reveling in the goodness of a stranger. Amanda's response was: "I feel so fortunate that I was chosen. What a gift to have the chance to potentially save someone's life."

After hearing about this selfless journey, I became curious about bone marrow donation. I found great information and many beautiful stories at BeTheMatch.org. This site also shares information about cord blood donation and how to organize a bone marrow donor registry drive.

As long as you're hanging around online, you might want

to take a look at OrganDonor.gov. Like Jacky and Jillian, organ donation can be done while we're living . . . or it can be our final act of kindness. Details on both types of donation are available on the site. You'll be amazed at what can be donated.

When kindness involves our sacred bodies, only we can know what makes sense for us and our families. The decision is always an individual choice. Some of us may choose to support these great organizations in other ways, perhaps through volunteering or through financial gifts. But the wise words of a plastic billboard outside a local church remind us of one type of organ donation that is a standing invitation for everyone. The sign said, "Be an organ donor. Give your heart to Jesus."

When we give our most vital organ to Jesus, we will hear His call and feel His nudge as we are clearly led to fulfill a need in His name. The need may not always require our body, but it will always require our love.

Share each other's burdens,
and in this way obey the law of Christ.
GALATIANS 6:2

CHAPTER 32

TIME AND TALENTS

CRUMBS ON THE BED from a delicious breakfast delivery. Hot coffee still in my hand, made with love by our youngest family member (best thing I ever taught that kid). A few flowers picked from a neglected, near-death plant on the back deck. And homemade cards, cherished and ready to stash in a special place. Forever. There I sat, thinking my homegrown Mother's Day wake-up call had concluded, when my daughter, Ellie, excitedly asked me to come downstairs for one more surprise.

I made my way curiously down the steps. To my great joy and disbelief, my super sweet, occasionally sassy, starting-to-notice-I'm-not-as-cool-as-I-once-thought-I-was teenager sat down at the piano.

She filled the room with beautiful music. My heart swelled at the sound of her voice singing the song I had recently fallen in love with. After all those years of my nagging the child to practice piano, she had taken it upon herself to learn my favorite song. And she gave it to me for Mother's Day.

Priceless.

Isn't it fascinating that our most valuable possessions don't cost a penny? They cost our time. Our God-given talents. If we want to wow someone with a unique gesture of kindness, we don't have to look any further than our own gifts and the precious minutes needed to share them.

My father-in-law is a woodworking genius. He can build just about anything. He uses this gift to connect with his grandkids, building memories right along with the physical items they create together. It isn't unusual to walk into his workshop when we're visiting to find my kids or my niece and nephew, Megan and Matt, hard at work under his close supervision. They have made baseball bats, napkin holders, doll beds, puzzles, benches, Christmas reindeer, tables, kaleidoscopes, bird houses, and toy airplanes. This grandpa is cultivating a special bond. He's teaching the kids new skills, and providing timeless memories with each glance at their creation. They have even used some of the projects for a cause, donating items to charitable silent auctions.

We each possess a special offering to bestow upon the world, a quality God has given us to glorify Him and serve one another. Do we know what our gifts are? Are we using them?

I once heard a story about a farmer with a beautifully manicured property. A friend stopped over and said, "God sure has blessed you." The farmer responded, "Yes, He has! But you should have seen this place when He was maintaining it Himself!"

God has much to offer us, but we play an important role in experiencing the fullness of His blessings. We are called to receive, refine, and reach out with our natural talents to enrich the lives of others.

Any kindness journey can be remarkably enhanced by looking deep into the well of our own talents and abilities. We can cook a delicious meal to share. Use our computer skills to help the technologically challenged. Make music. Draw a picture and mail it to a loved one. Plant a garden. Be a Sunday school teacher. Tutor a classmate. French braid a friend's hair. Organize a fundraiser. Write a poem. Take pictures. Read with a child. Build something. Sign up to coach. Listen. Paint a room. Bake for a graduation, wedding, funeral, or just because. Make a flower arrangement. Help someone master a skill. Share knowledge. Offer a good eye for decorating. Be a mentor. Knit scarves and put them in public places for whoever needs one (with a kindness card and a note that says "made just for you").

Receiving an act of kindness through someone's natural talent is memorable and moving. It's a perfect reminder that we all have a special gift to share.

One Thursday morning, I walked out of my Bible study meeting into the glory of a luminous spring day. As soon as I descended the stairs of the church and headed toward my car, I heard the delicate sound of soothing music. I wasn't even sure where it was coming from.

And then I saw him. A young man in ripped jeans and a plain white T-shirt. He was sitting under a tree, strumming his guitar, and releasing his gift of music into the air for anyone to enjoy. Two hundred women attend that meeting, not to mention the children in tow. And he was ministering to us, voluntarily, with no other motive than to share the blessing God had entrusted to him. The song he was singing, "Good, Good Father," by Chris Tomlin, stayed with me throughout the day. And to this very moment, when I hear that song I think of him. His willingness to share his talent. His kindness.

God has placed vibrant confetti in our hands, will we close our fingers tightly around it, or boldly release it into the air?

In his grace, God has given us different gifts for doing certain things well. So if God has given you the ability to prophesy, speak out with as much faith as God has given you. If your gift is serving others, serve them well. If you are a teacher, teach well. If your gift is to encourage others, be encouraging. If it is giving, give generously. If God has given you leadership ability, take the responsibility seriously. And if you have a gift for showing kindness to others, do it gladly.

ROMANS 12:6–8

CHAPTER 33

PRAISE FOR
OUR POTTERS

MY KIDS WALKED INTO THE HOUSE as if it was no big deal for them to be there. "Hey, Papa. Hi, Nonna," they said casually. After a quick double take, the combination of total shock and exuberant joy on my parents' faces brought us all to laughter. I would drive seven hours on the mind-numbing Pennsylvania Turnpike any time for that reaction!

I couldn't possibly have a forty-day birthday celebration without doing something big for the awesome people responsible for my birth. A surprise visit was the kids' idea, and man, did they get it right. Day 27 was a winner for everyone involved.

As I lay awake in bed that night in my childhood home, I found myself running through a mental slideshow: clip after clip, celebrating my parents and the other people I was incredibly fortunate to have surrounding me in my youth. Grandparents. Aunts and uncles. Cousins. Close friends. Leading me to where I am, to who I am. Shaping me and molding me, like potters to clay. Not all perfect moments, of course, because that's not real life . . . but good moments. So much goodness. Countless reasons to rejoice.

In my experience, these beautiful *potters* are far too easy to take for granted. While I certainly acknowledge the work of their hands, I seldom stop to express sincere appreciation. Even with a fullness of heartfelt gratitude, I rarely take time to craft words that capture my emotions and praise their impact on my life. Looking back, I most vividly remember three times that I committed to digging deep into my soul to honor extraordinary lives—lives that influenced me tremendously. All three times, those words were memorials, celebrations of lives well lived. And all three times my reflections held sentiments I wish I had said *to* my loved ones, not *about* them.

I'd like to offer up a kindness challenge for all of us. Let's think of a *potter* in our life, someone who has played a major role in sculpting our story or our character, and create a tribute to present to that person. If you don't like to write or you're not exactly eloquent, that's okay! As long as it's from the heart, it will be perfect.

A tribute is a presentation of honest, thoughtful words meant to honor someone important to us. It's a great reason to use fancy paper and a document frame. We can start with a favorite story and then include admired virtues, treasured and humorous memories, traditions we hope to continue, applause for how they changed our life, and sincere words of thanks.

If you're a fan of the Broadway musical *Wicked*, you might have the lyrics from the song "For Good" playing in your head: "Because I knew you, I have been changed for good." This is the message a tribute conveys, a message that is sure to touch a heart. Through earnest, honest words, we can create a gift that will be cherished, saved, and passed on.

During my teenage years, I had a certain fondness for writing poems. Rhymey sing-songy, mediocre poems. I can remember the mess of papers scattered across my desk and a Rolodex of words spinning through my head. I'd sit for hours trying to get each line just right. When one of my closest friends (one of my potters) was leaving for college, I created a poem for her before she left. I expressed my deepest gratitude, poured out my heart, celebrated our friendship, and recapped our "greatest hits." I typed it out on an electric typewriter, beautified it with a squiggled purple border, and gently placed it in a clear box frame. I couldn't wait to give it to her.

Recently, I called my triple-decade bestie, envisioning the project prominently displayed in her dorm room. I asked if she still had it. Without pause, she said, "Have it? I have most of that thing memorized! I probably read it a million times during college. That frame has traveled with me every single place I've lived for the past twenty-five years."

I wouldn't have given it a label at the time, but that poem was a tribute. And it was time well spent.

The sentiment behind our words far surpasses their quality. Our dedication of time and effort can serve a beautiful purpose in another person's life. It creates a legacy in their honor, for their honor.

The tributes I wrote as memorials did not reach the ears of my beloved grandparents and a forever-in-my-heart friend, but I'm sincerely thankful for the words that capture the essence of their lives and their enormous impact on me. The process of reflecting and creating this labor of love is therapeutic, and the finished product is a treasure. So don't worry if your potter is no longer with you; you can still write a spectacular tribute. Share it with family members or friends, hang it in a special place, print it in the newspaper, or post it on social media for a special anniversary.

While God is our first and ultimate potter (Isaiah 64:8), He has strategically placed many people throughout our lives to help us take shape. They are the people who teach, heal, guide, inspire, empower, restore, and love us. People who will glow at the sight of our written words. A sincere tribute. Praise for our *potters*.

And now, dear brothers and sisters, one final thing.
Fix your eyes on what is true, and honorable, and right,
and pure, and lovely, and admirable.
Think about things that are excellent and worthy of praise.
PHILIPPIANS 4:8

CHAPTER 34

BLESSED EARTH

IN MY HUMBLE MATERNAL OPINION, my child was well on his way to a prosperous engineering career. The block structures he created took us by surprise. It was a passion he carried over to free-play at school, as we received e-mailed photos of the masterpieces from his intrigued kindergarten teacher. Bridges. Skyscrapers. Castles. All strategically designed and carefully constructed, often boasting a blueprint drawn out in advance.

But our resident builder had a major problem while he was working under our roof. The problem was an adorable, rambunctious terror, standing under three feet tall. Milk mustache . . . mischievous smirk. He'd knock down anything in his path.

Between toppled towers, puddles of tears, and an occasionally tackled toddler, the tension in our house was steadily growing. "Brotherly love" wasn't going so well in this season of life.

Reasoning with a two-year-old is no small feat, but I did my best. I was determined to teach the importance of showing love through respecting the work of others. I continually reminded our little tornado to be nice to his brother by being nice to his brother's special things. Slowly, the situation started to improve. It wasn't perfect, but it was progress.

Do you ever wonder if God experiences similar frustrations regarding His beautiful creation? His meticulous design. His gift to us. Does He ever wish we would be more attentive, more committed to caring for our earth?

Genesis 1:31 reveals God's pride as He observes His awesome work of art, "Then God looked over all he had made, and he saw that it was very good!"

As a reflection of our love for God, we are called to show the same love toward His marvelous creation and everything in it. We should leave the world better than it was when we arrived, tending to our one and only earth for the sake of those who come next, savoring the magnificence of nature.

Like the vast expanse of our planet, the responsibility of taking care of a whole environment is immense. The mere thought of it may overwhelm us—how could one person possibly make an impact?—and allow us to settle for complacency or inaction. But while we certainly can't do it alone, many people making small changes can lead to enormous gain.

One concerned teenager did a meaningful project through an organization called Kids for Positive Change (kidsforpositivechange.com). She wanted to share the importance of caring for our planet and our sea life through committing to reusable bags.

Sea turtles in particular are not big fans of plastic bags because they fatally mistake them for jellyfish and eat them. The results are heartbreaking. So this teen set out to teach small groups of kids how to make reusable bags using old T-shirts. She taught "T-shirt Transformation" to friends, scout troops, classrooms, and youth groups.

Making a reusable bag is a fun activity for Forty Days of Kindness. The bags really couldn't be simpler to create. Here's how: Start with a T-shirt turned inside out (an adult medium or large works well). Lay the shirt flat on a table. Cut off the sleeves on the seam. Cut around the neck opening so the opening is evenly scooped on both sides. This makes the handles of the bag. At this point, the shirt looks like a tank top with a scoop neck in the front and back. Close up the bottom of the T-shirt by tying it with a rubber band. Flip the shirt back to the right side. And . . . *tada*!

We could easily fill up our fancy reusable bag with great ideas on how to care for our earth: Recycle. Turn off lights and water. Go paperless wherever possible. Commit to reusable grocery bags and reusable water bottles. Carpool. Organize a "Green Team" with kids to educate and empower the next generation. Plant trees. Start a compost pile—learn how at gardeningknowhow.org. Pick up litter. Plan a litter scavenger hunt on Earth Day. Switch to LED lightbulbs to save energy. Fix water and energy leaks in our homes. Unplug electronic devices when they're fully charged. Paint or add bling to recycling bins to make them more eye-catching. Collect old newspapers for a local animal shelter. Foster an animal. Give a unique gift to honor a loved one and support nature at nature. org—sea turtle nests, migratory bird resting areas, even orangutan family forests! Make a bird feeder or a birdhouse. Volunteer at an arboretum, an animal care organization, or a local organic farm. Challenge friends and family to an electricity-free day. Play outside at every age. Enjoy the exquisite beauty of nature!

Such simple suggestions squeeze easily right into our lives, yet I admit to dropping the ball on many of these responsibilities. I absentmindedly leave my reusable bags in the car at the grocery store, let the water run while I brush my teeth, and occasionally forget to turn off a light when I leave a room. But with our hearts tuned in to kindness, it's a perfect time to reflect on small tweaks to our lives that could significantly impact our collective home.

If we join hands to encircle our blessed earth, we can keep the tower from toppling. We can love God by loving His work, His creation.

Let the heavens be glad, and the earth rejoice!
Let the sea and everything in it shout his praise!
Let the fields and their crops burst out with joy!
Let the trees of the forest sing for joy before the LORD!
PSALM 96:11–13

CHAPTER 35

SAY YES

I WAS CLANGING THROUGH pots and pans as I raced to start dinner when muffled ringing and a caller ID announcement stopped me in my tracks. The robotic voice declared, "University. Of. Dayton."

Ah. Those familiar words always brought a twinge of warm nostalgia for my college days. Instant memories of a nurturing home that left me with many reasons for gratitude—particularly the world's sweetest friends . . . now scattered across the country.

Unfortunately, that oozing of emotion didn't typically motivate me to pick up the phone with my credit card in hand. Usually, I just smiled and went back to whatever task I was in the middle of completing.

But this evening, day sixteen of daily kindness, I decided to press pause on my dinner prep and say yes to the interruption.

The student on the other end of the call was a sunny upper-classman beginning to look at counseling programs. A great start to the conversation, as I answered some questions, listened to her dreams, and shared my own experiences and encouragement. I wondered how many engaging chats with fellow Flyers I had missed out on over the years, unwilling to stop what I was doing for a few minutes to say yes.

Yes.

It's an intricate word that can make us tremble or cheer; it can open doors to muddy uncertainty as well as possibilities beyond our wildest imagination.

We are taught to protect ourselves by learning to say no. We're cautioned against no-no's like people pleasing and overcommitting. But we aren't being encouraged to say no to everything. Rather, the objective is to save space in our lives so we can say yes to the best things.

In my own experience, even a simple yes can unexpectedly trip me up, and I tiptoe away instead with a knee-jerk *not today*. Saying no can easily become a comfortable autopilot reaction, leaving us unwilling to head into unchartered waters or power through feelings of hesitation.

If you're with me, I'd like to offer up a *yes challenge*, a chance to practice yessing while we're out there spreading kindness. By intentionally focusing on *yes*, perhaps we can start to lose the instinctive *no*. You know, the one that can keep us from joy and growth. Would you be willing, just for one day, to commit to saying yes to everything good that comes your way? (Notice, I have provided an opportunity for your first yes!)

Yes to the volunteer position that's been sitting on your heart. *Yes* to reading an extra chapter with the kids at bedtime. *Yes* to a conversation with the new student at school. *Yes* to bumping out the wall of your comfort zone. *Yes* to a favor on a crazy busy day. *Yes* when your sibling asks for the last cookie. *Yes* to an evening out when you'd rather just relax in pajamas. *Yes* to the donation jar for charity. *Yes* to giving someone a chance. *Yes* to forgiveness.

I took the challenge and spent a day saying yes to all good things. During the very first hour, a friend texted me and asked if I could get together that afternoon. She wanted to quickly go through some things for a project we were working on. My thumbs immediately started to click the reasons I wouldn't be able to swing it. The day was already pretty jammed. Remembering my commitment to yes, I deleted my answer, looked closely at my calendar, and found a window of time to meet with her.

As it turned out, she was having a super lousy day. Spending time together was exactly what she needed. And because I had the chance to be a sounding board for her, I was then able to keep her in my prayers and reach out later to see how she was doing. These valuable moments grow a relationship and wrap our people in the certainty of our love.

All because I changed my answer from *not today* to *yes*.

Pushing ourselves outside our comfort zone with intentional yesses will reveal unexpected opportunities for kindness. If we're looking for a supercharge of strength for this challenge, we can find it in the biggest, boldest, most blessed yes—a rooftop yes to God.

Saying yes to God's love and to His Word enables us to say yes to God's plan. The most dependable way to honor others is through living out God's purpose for our lives. We can give Him our very first yes every day by recommitting to His will and re-affirming our trust in His promises.

Beginning with that first yes of the morning, saying yes can change our outlook and our direction. Staying alert for *yes moments* during the day is a unique approach to kindness. It is reactive. Organic. It moves us along a path we didn't pave. Things are sure to stay interesting when we don't plan ahead for kindness. Instead, we just say yes and see where we land!

For no matter how many promises God has made,
they are "Yes" in Christ.
And so through him the "Amen" is spoken
by us to the glory of God.
2 CORINTHIANS 1:20 NIV

CHAPTER 36

UPSIDE-DOWN KINDNESS

I REMEMBER SEEING HER at church, interacting casually when we picked up our kids from the nursery. There was a pleasant presence about her. She was one of those people you just feel good to be around. Someone you admire simply by observing her interactions with others. An acquaintance you know will evolve into a friend.

And now . . . through a decade of friendship and hours upon hours of conversation, my admiration for my dear sister in Christ has only grown. There is one unique characteristic about her that quietly astounds me in this sacred relationship.

I have never heard her say a negative word about anyone. Ever. It simply doesn't happen.

As a work in progress in this area, I seek to emulate her, imagining a peaceful freedom in separating myself from all things resembling gossip.

I observe her role as a listener in groups. She remains humbly disengaged from shining a light on people's flaws. I have a heightened sense of comfort confiding in her, knowing without question that my blotches and blemishes are safe in her care. I relish our conversations. Conversations wrapped up in ideas, solutions, and connection; conversations free of that uneasy feeling following negative words or words that aren't ours to share.

Thinking through this silent act of love, I called her to talk about this interpersonal awesomeness. She was flattered and surprised that I had noticed her restraint, and she admitted that controlling her words isn't always easy. This virtue in her is not accidental. It is very much intentional. She chooses to treat others as she would like to be treated. She acknowledges the sting of disrespectful words and honors the age-old adage, "If you don't have something nice to say, don't say anything."

My treasured friend flips kindness on its head. Rather than *doing something* to show kindness, she *refrains from doing something* to show kindness. She loves others through a kind spirit, keeping her hands perfectly still. This upside-down kindness doesn't require any additional time in our schedules; rather, it calls us to attention. Kindness by being, not by doing. It invites us to take a closer look at how we relate and respond to people; it encourages us to look honestly at ourselves, to open our eyes to attitude shifts, to identify possible renovations to our hearts that can heal, bless, and ripple! Upside-down kindness takes serving others a step beyond action; it highlights who we are and what we stand for.

One thing has always been clear regarding our relationships with others: We can't control the thoughts or behavior of other people. Total bummer. However, we *can* control our side of the equation. When we change our response, our attitude, our approach, we can make a world of difference in alleviating tension in ourselves and in others.

Sometimes this change of heart can be as simple as giving the benefit of the doubt. I recently called a family member with an apology for something I had said. I didn't intend to be offensive, but after I replayed the conversation in my head, I was concerned that I could have been misunderstood. My family member responded with, "That didn't even cross my mind. I always assume positive intent."

Assume positive intent.

Because this philosophy was put into action, I can no longer remember any details of the feared misunderstanding; it was completely erased by a loving response and a positive attitude. More than likely, if there had been a confrontation or the assumption of negative intent, the memories would be lit up on some internal billboard, causing annoyed physical reactions with every thought.

Positive energy can also take effect when we swallow unpleasant words ready to fly out of our mouths. An eleven-year-old girl who participated in Forty Days of Kindness inquired precisely about upside-down kindness. She asked if "not doing something" counts as kindness. When asked for clarification, the child shared that her brother had worn a ridiculous outfit to school that day (complete with a construction-paper bow tie taped to his shirt), and she had deliberately chosen not to tell him how weird he looked.

First Peter 3:11 instructs us to "search for peace, and work to maintain it." From the magnitude of world peace to the most basic peace within our own homes, living harmoniously is hard work. Undeniably. And while resolution may seem impossible at times, there is usually something we can reframe or something from which we can refrain, to create harmony.

Instead of judging, love. Instead of criticizing, give grace. Instead of jealousy, choose joy. Instead of complaining, show gratitude. Instead of arrogance, be humble. Instead of resentment, forgive. Instead of impatience, seek understanding. Instead of anger, embrace peace. Instead of condemning, pray. Instead of gossip, share success. Instead of dishonesty, speak truth. Instead of rejection, invite.

The absence of negative tendencies on the inside can't help but show up on the outside. That is precisely what I was drawn to in the church nursery all those years ago, observing my pure-hearted friend just going about her day.

Upside-down kindness nourishes our character and equips us to share Christ's love simply by showing up!

May God, who gives this patience and encouragement,
help you live in complete harmony with each other,
as is fitting for followers of Christ Jesus.
ROMANS 15:5

CHAPTER 37

THE HEART OF HOMELESSNESS

I DROVE AWAY FROM the community center with a full heart and curious ears, waiting for a reaction from my kids about their experience. We had spent the afternoon volunteering at a holiday party, creating crafts with homeless families and families recovering from homelessness.

With over eighty guests at the event and volunteers of all ages, the party room was hopping! It was filled with craft stations, face painting, dancing, delicious food, and an exciting visit from Santa. My kids had led an ornament-making craft station, and they'd even jumped on the dance floor when the DJ played "Macarena."

We had often talked about people in need, shopped for children at Christmas, and given donations, but this was the first time the kids had the privilege of serving directly in this way. Seeking to start a dialogue with them, a question popped into my head, "Did anything surprise you today?" Without a moment of hesitation, my daughter eagerly blurted out these words, "If it weren't for the name tags, I wouldn't have known which kids were helpers and which kids were homeless. We're the same."

We were all quiet for a moment, absorbing this precise observation, then everyone chimed in with similar thoughts, sharing stories about the kids at the party, using their names, excited to volunteer again. Any initial uneasiness had been replaced by unity and understanding.

Children have a way of untangling a complex world with their purity of heart and mind. They look right past the labels we often place on each other.

The word *homelessness* can bring a stereotyped image to mind, which is sometimes followed by judgment or even fear. But if we look past the name tag and straight to the beating heart of the person in front of us, we will see far more similarities than differences.

I recently had the privilege of talking with a team of women from a nonprofit organization, the Friends Association for the Care and Protection of Children (friendsassoc.org), a group working tirelessly to end family homelessness. I noticed something about their language throughout our conversation. They referred to their clients as "people experiencing homelessness," "families experiencing homelessness," and "children experiencing homelessness." *Homelessness* did not come first. Before anything else, we are people, God's people.

When we interact with people who are homeless, reflecting this truth is the greatest gift we can give. We must seek to truly see them, not just look at them. Smile. Say hello. Offer respect. Engage in conversation. Learn their names. Offer kindness instead of making assumptions. In short, we use the same standards of quality we have for ourselves.

The circumstances that lead to homelessness are often beyond our comprehension. But reaching out to help doesn't require understanding; all that is needed is a willingness to show love. From one person to another.

A teenager named Steven had a newfound heart for the homeless. He'd been in the city with his uncle for a sporting event and, with his uncle taking the lead, they made a last-minute change in their dinner plans. They bought dinner for three from a street vendor and sat down on a park bench for a meal and a conversation with a homeless man named Ken.

This simple interaction had such an impact on Steven that he decided to incorporate helping the homeless into his Forty Days of Kindness project. He led his very willing basketball team in making homeless care packages. The players signed up to bring different items for the packages, and the team got together to fill Ziploc freezer bags with the goods.

The bags included items like granola bars, sunscreen, wet wipes, tissues, lip balm, hand warmers, toiletries, socks, gloves, Band-Aids, notes of encouragement, and gift cards for food. Once the bags were assembled, the team members each took two bags. They planned to keep them in their cars or in their parents' cars, so when they came upon a person in need, they would be ready.

Such an incredible way to unite a team and extend the reach and the spirit of kindness!

If you choose to create care packages, individually or with a group, you could also include a card to share information about the phone number 2-1-1. This is a national, free service that is available 24-7 to help people find local resources for just about anything related to human services. Anyone can dial those three numbers at any time and connect with a person who can help to meet needs such as food, healthcare, job support, and housing. Check out 211.org to learn more.

When we stop to have a conversation with a person who is homeless, we open a door to discovering specifically how we can help. We can ask directly if there is something they need in that moment. Imagine the difference that can be made if we're able to meet an urgent request: maybe a pair of warm boots, a sleeping bag, or a prepaid cell phone.

Beyond face-to-face contact with the homeless population, we can offer our help and financial support through local agencies. Dedicated agencies are peppered across the country, offering resources and empowerment, filling in the gaps of a support network, and passionately working to break the cycle of homelessness. A few examples of national websites that can lead to local organizations are: endhomelessness.org, nationalhomelessness.org, and standupforkids.org.

As the meeting with my friends at the Friends Association closed, the Director of Development, Robin Meixner, emphasized the importance of mentoring, refraining from judgment, and simply being present. She said, "My job is to help others be the very best they can be."

Regardless of our "name tag," with or without an address, everyone deserves to be their personal best. What can we do to help?

Therefore if you have any encouragement from being united
with Christ, if any comfort from his love, if any common sharing
in the Spirit, if any tenderness and compassion,
then make my joy complete by being like-minded,
having the same love, being one in spirit and of one mind.
Do nothing out of selfish ambition or vain conceit.
Rather, in humility value others above yourselves,
not looking to your own interests but each of you to the interests
of others. In your relationships with one another,
have the same mindset as Christ Jesus.

PHILIPPIANS 2:1–5 NIV

CHAPTER 38

GET WELL SOON

AT AGE TWENTY-FIVE, six months before our wedding day, a thyroid cancer diagnosis felt like a giant piece of fondant wedding cake straight to the face. This was not on the playlist. In fact, it was an abrupt stop to the music altogether, leaving us frozen in our tracks. Shocked. Quiet.

In my usual, stubborn, I'll-do-it-my-way style, I refused to push back the wedding date. The doctors were on board, and there was no changing my mind. Perhaps I needed to keep one hand on the future, on the life we had been dreaming about.

Two surgeries and my treatment plan got squeezed between dress fittings and menu selections. And it was just as you might imagine. It stunk. It was hard. It was scary. It was discouraging. It was exhausting. It was painful.

And yet, throughout my struggle, the people rallying around me continually enabled me and my family to feel blessed. Not necessarily blessed by the circumstance, but blessed by their love.

Like the morning sun rising over a mountain, every little act of kindness revealed more and more light each day. Small gestures like a card, a prayer, a phone call, a visit, or a hug were often exactly what was needed to keep going.

Even with this insider information, even having lived it myself, I still catch myself backing away sometimes when people in my life are sick. I worry I'll get it wrong. I'm unsure of what to do or say. But once I take the first step to reach out, it becomes clear that there really isn't a right or wrong way to help. We don't need to be perfect—it's often enough just to be present.

About a week after my first thyroid surgery where they removed a growth and half of the thyroid, I was feeling fine. I planned to go to my follow-up doctor appointment alone. My friends and family had been all hands on deck, and I was happy to handle this one on my own. Besides, it was just a quick follow-up. I was certain the pathology report would be clear, and I could get on with life.

At the last minute, one of my coworkers heard about this plan of mine, and she absolutely insisted that she would be taking me. She took the rest of the day off work, and drove me to the city for my appointment. *The appointment.* The one where I was told, even to the surgeon's surprise, that the mass was malignant. I was not at the end of the detour after all. I was at the beginning.

My friend's hand was like a rare diamond that day. I held on tight with no intention of letting go. She used her other hand to write down everything the doctors were saying, important information I could not begin to wrap my head around. And then she drove me home.

I have no doubt that the Holy Spirit was at work that morning, and I've never been more thankful for the gift of a faithful, persistent friend.

As we listen for God's guidance and seek ways to help a loved one who is sick, small gestures can make an enormous difference. Enormous.

We can send frequent notes or texts. Share the number of a friend who can be a resource. Research local support groups. Make or organize meals. Listen. Act as a traveling spa service—give a manicure or pedicure. Provide a break and encouragement to the caregivers. Stop over or call to read a chapter of a book, something fun to look forward to daily or weekly. Share a funny story. Send pictures of events that had to be missed. Send a care package. Play with the kids or be the chauffeur. Instead of asking what you can do, ask what needs to be done. Call to see if you can stop by for a visit. Pray! Participate in a charity run or bike ride for their cause. Research wellness and nutrition information to share; check out the Education and Resources tabs on UniteforHer.org. Let them know about medgift.com, an organization that makes it easier to ask for help—it works like a bridal or baby registry, providing opportunities for loved ones to help with care, financial needs, and wish lists. Offer to maintain a website to update friends and family on caringbridge.org.

Beyond what we may imagine, our willingness to show up and

show compassion can be a lifeline during an illness. When our bodies are weak, our spirits crave strength. The love and kindness of others provide the most powerful fuel.

Therefore we do not lose heart. Though outwardly we are wasting away, yet inwardly we are being renewed day by day. For our light and momentary troubles are achieving for us an eternal glory that far outweighs them all. So we fix our eyes not on what is seen, but on what is unseen, since what is seen is temporary, but what is unseen is eternal.

2 Corinthians 4:16–18 niv

CHAPTER 39

SHARPENED FOR SUCCESS

DETERMINATION WAS WRITTEN all over the little boy's bright red face as he firmly gripped his parents' hands. Cautiously, with quick, wobbly steps, the family made their way around the ice rink. Again and again and again, until finally, the courageous boy let go and glided off on his own, protected by a powder-blue Mickey Mouse helmet and full snow gear. If you're picturing an ice skating prodigy launching into a sensational spin with applause from the crowd . . . that's not what happened. The kid fell about a hundred times. But his parents helped him up, gave him gentle instruction, and cheered him on as he kept going.

Stumbling nearby, at the same open-skate session, was a grown woman on the exact same mission. Minus the Mickey helmet. A friend held her by the arm, slowly escorting her around the unfamiliar, slippery surface. Like a child taking her first steps, she was unyielding in her quest for success, but it wasn't easy. And she couldn't do it alone.

I stood on the sideline, warming my body with steaming hot chocolate, and I reflected on this image, this reminder of our ever-present need for support. Through each stage of life, we encounter fresh challenges, some by choice and others by necessity. Unchartered ground often requires backup—someone to walk beside us, hold us up, lift us when we fall, and give us a high five when we make it.

Glancing attentively around the ice rink of our daily lives, we can start to identify people who are inching along, holding firm to the wall while they gain momentum. Can we offer a steady hand? A reassuring presence? A word of encouragement? A nudge toward success?

Proverbs 27:17 says, "As iron sharpens iron, so a friend sharpens a friend." When we commit to helping others succeed, we are doing God's work. We are bringing out the best in people so they can bring their best to the world.

We can teach a skill we have that someone else needs. Study with someone struggling in class. Support and promote a new business or a service project. Openly share valuable resources. Walk closely beside someone dealing with a life-altering loss or a health struggle. Take the new person at work under our wing. Invite a friend to Bible study. Connect two friends who can help each other. Support the person making healthy eating or lifestyle choices. Offer to run with someone training for that first big race. Congratulate a victory even when it results in our defeat, knowing we can trust God to have great plans for us too.

Traveling alongside others as a champion for their success can be an exceptional business model. Every time I've seen a business committed to helping others, it has left a lasting impression.

For example, I know a photographer who dedicates one month of her earnings each year to a scholarship fund for underprivileged kids in her community. Her clients make their checks directly to the fund, and they often round up. Way up!

During a weekend visit to New York City many years ago, my husband and I met a man who took his hair salon on the road, giving haircuts on the street to men and women in need. Unforgettable.

A dry-cleaner compassionately uses his business to serve others, offering to help the unemployed population by cleaning interview clothing for free. His gesture reaches beyond the clients he supports and catches the eyes of all who see his sign announcing this offer. It's a sign that reminds us that there are good people everywhere. A sign that celebrates our capacity to show kindness in unexpected ways.

Ryan, a dad leading his two kids on a kindness journey, also observed an exceptional business model that is changing lives. One of their favorite acts of kindness was going to a one-dollar pizza shop in Philadelphia called Rosa's Fresh Pizza (rosasfreshpizza. com). The owner, Mason Wartman, began a pay-it-forward system where people can purchase a slice of pizza for someone who is homeless. The customer pays for an extra slice of pizza, and then puts a colorful sticky note on the wall to represent the free slice. The notes are filled with words of love and encouragement.

When a homeless person comes into the pizza shop, they can grab a sticky note off the wall as their payment and enjoy a delicious slice of pizza. They don't have to ask for help. Rather, they are made to feel welcome, delightfully able to interact with others as equals.

On a thank-you note posted on the wall, one homeless patron exclaimed that he was about to begin a new job. He was grateful to everyone at Rosa's for the support to get back on his feet. He shared, "Everybody wants the world to change, but for that to happen, we have to change ourselves."

Rosa's feeds between thirty and forty homeless people every day!

Whether we have a business or we're simply in the business of showing kindness, a little creativity can result in exciting ways to keep others standing and thriving. We can rejoice equally in our own success and in the success of others by using our gifts to enhance theirs, joining hands, and striving to make everyone shine for the glory of God.

Therefore encourage one another and build each other up, just as in fact you are doing.
1 THESSALONIANS 5:11 NIV

CHAPTER 40

THINK BIG

I WALKED DOWNSTAIRS to find an enormous birthday banner garnishing our sliding door. My parents had sent this fun monstrosity weeks in advance, and asked the kids to hang it up on my big day. The big 4–0. The much anticipated milestone had arrived, and that meant it was also the fortieth day of kindness!

When my youngest son realized this connection, he began to fret: "But we never did anything for the college kids. I really wanted to do something nice for the college kids." I assured him that we would continue to do acts of kindness even though the official project was ending. He wasn't satisfied with that answer. He was determined to drop some kindness on our local university. Immediately.

I put my kindness plan for the day on hold and let the child lead the charge; he said he had already thought it through and decided to give a soft pretzel to every single person on the campus! *Whew.* That order would certainly rock the world of the pretzel shop! We compromised, bought one hundred soft pretzels, and took them to one of the residence halls.

I looked back in my Forty Days of Kindness Journal to find a detailed description of the day, complete with these closing words, "We left some kindness cards and off we went, hand in hand with huge smiles on our faces. Great finale and a sacred moment I know I will remember always."

Reflecting on that unexpected act of kindness, I admire my son's ambition to do it up. A *let's feed everyone* attitude. If he'd learned anything in forty days, it was that, even at age six, he could make a difference in the world. He was empowered. He was thinking big!

Small acts of kindness are spectacular, undeniably, but we may sometimes feel moved to kick it up a notch. Whatever we can do for one, we can do for many.

A friend and her six-year-old daughter challenged themselves to collect 20,000 pounds of nonperishable food for local food banks in one year.

With a glowing face painted in chocolate ice cream and the melodic tune of the ice cream truck fading into the distance, a giggling child shared how one grown-up had bought a treat for every kid in the neighborhood.

A few women in our county collaborated to start a chapter of an organization called 100+ Women Who Care (100womenwho-carecc.org). Four times each year, these ladies bring together one hundred women (each with $100), and they donate $10,000 to a local charity. That's $40,000 each year going directly into their own community! It's a great concept to replicate wherever you are.

Inspired by the life of Eleanor Roosevelt, a small group of middle school students and their teacher started a Kindness Club called WWED (What Would Eleanor Do?). The group fills the halls with sunshine, making tear-off compliment posters, leaving positive notes on lockers and tucked into library books, giving out *kindness coins* to students caught being kind, posting encouraging signs throughout the school, and inspiring more kindness.

When we're out there scattering goodness, let's keep a lookout for these supercharged moments. Look for ways to extend God's love beyond our original intention. With fistfuls of seeds thrown into the wind, the bloom of kindness is infinite!

Thinking big for kindness can also mean doing or being something big for one person. My brother's best friend, Matt, would tell you that my dad was that person for him. That big presence. The filler of a void.

Raised by a wonderful, hardworking, single mom, Matt did not have a relationship with his dad. When Matt entered our lives at age six, the whole idea of a dad was foreign to him, but he quickly found a father figure. My dad welcomed him into our home and into his heart, always treating Matt like one of the family and helping to guide him through life.

At Matt's wedding reception, he opened up to another mentor and friend, the priest who celebrated the big day. Matt revealed a complete lack of ideas on how to adequately express thanks for something so big. He credited my dad, along with many other key players, for the life he was leading. For the ability to make the good choices that kept him on a straight path. For gifts of unconditional love and support. How do you say thank you for that, he wondered. The answer he received became guiding words that he continues to carry with him, "Sometimes you don't need to say anything, sometimes the best thank-you is trying to be more like them."

And so the ripples continue. Matt heads out into the world remembering all the virtues and qualities that have blessed him, and he seeks to keep those values going. He shares more kindness; pays it forward. Ready to intentionally impact a life, fill in a gap, and love others on purpose.

If I speak in the tongues of men or of angels, but do not have love,
I am only a resounding gong or a clanging cymbal.

1 Corinthians 13:1 NIV

CONCLUSION

IGNITE KINDNESS!

I DID SOMETHING FOOLISH as I approached the finish line of this book-writing project. Unintentional. But foolish.

Remember the chapter about self-care? And the one about putting people before projects? And the words celebrating the amazing guidance and power of the Holy Spirit?

Yeah. All those things. Thrown to the side.

At some point, without even realizing it, I had put my head down and started to sprint. I stopped taking time to refuel. I let go of anything that didn't involve writing or meeting the basic needs of my family. And I'm sad to say that I even left Jesus in my dust, with a dismissive wave saying, "Thanks, but I can take it from here."

The result? It wasn't pretty. I fell hard.

Flat.

On.

My.

Face.

With every physical, emotional, spiritual, and mental resource thoroughly depleted, what remained was a sick, sleepless, anxious mess.

Not exactly how I had seen things playing out.

It took a little while to stand up and dust myself off, but eventually I wobbled back onto the course. Slow and steady, cautiously keeping my balance.

As I worked to restore myself and get back into the full spirit of writing, I dug out my original kindness journal, seeking inspiration from the notes I kept during my forty-day birthday celebration. My very first words on this topic were right in front of me, handwritten, beneath the hardback, subtle gold journal cover.

On day four, I wrote: "I'm realizing how often I miss opportunities to show kindness because I'm always racing to the next thing. I need to consciously start slowing down and keep perspective on what really matters. Acts of kindness can take just a few minutes, but they leave an impact that can last a lifetime."

I reflected on my starting point, the initial experience of excitement and gratitude for acts of kindness. I relished the stories and the insights in my journal, many of which I have shared in these pages. And I decided to travel full circle and get back to a daily kindness practice. I figured the best way to reconnect with the power of kindness is through kindness.

It was no surprise that I immediately began feeling blessed by giving, but the blessings were much different this time around. Acts of kindness shared during a time of brokenness revealed a whole new experience. Reaching out with love from an empty well proved to be a beautiful path to a refill.

Paired with a recommitment to prayer, and a great doctor, daily acts of kindness played a huge role in reviving my spirit and my health. Renewed. Refreshed.

When we turn our attention away from our own struggles and focus on what we can offer others, we come face-to-face with the healing qualities of kindness. We find meaning and strength through serving because it reminds us of what we *have* rather than what we *lack*.

And that is yet another way to enrich our own lives by pouring into the people around us.

I wonder about your experience—I'm curious if you've implemented kindness practices into your day. Maybe something unexpected has crept into your journey too. What have you discovered? Has it changed you or your family? Has your soul been fed as you've nourished others? Perhaps scattering kindness has served you as a healer, a teacher, an eye-opener, an energizer, or an answered prayer.

Whether you've always engaged in acts of kindness, you've recently started focusing more on kindness (maybe with a forty-day kindness commitment), or you're just getting started, I pray that you experience a boomerang of joy. Richly blessed by the extension of your hand in loving service.

While we don't typically set out to give in order to receive, there is no denying the profound benefits to our own lives, our own hearts. Ephesians 2:10 clarifies why we are lifted up by reaching out: "For we are God's handiwork, created in Christ Jesus to do good works, which God prepared in advance for us to do" (NIV).

Created in Christ Jesus to do good works.

We were designed for spreading kindness! No wonder it feels so good.

When we use our time, our talents, and our resources to make a difference in the lives of other people, we are fulfilling the very purpose of our existence.

The win-win nature of kindness is baked right into the recipe. We provide help, encouragement, and love to others—enriching their lives as well as our own. We witness the life-giving impact we can make, even in the smallest ways, by turning someone's bad day into a good one. We feel joyful in our giving and we keep going, scattering more seeds of Christ's love, empowered by our work as His hands and feet. The recipients of our acts of kindness are inspired to pass on the blessings, and the ripples continue. Love rains. Love reigns.

It's exhilarating to think about the difference we can make in our lives and in the world through this simple practice. Together we can change the atmosphere. We can create a contagious outbreak of kindness. And as we've seen throughout these *forty ways to love and inspire others*, acts of kindness can fit right into a typical day, right into our busy schedules.

We wouldn't jump to this conclusion by turning on the evening news, but there is already a remarkable amount of goodness surrounding us. People across our communities and across continents are embracing their fellow brothers and sisters in marvelous ways. Simple gestures of compassion. Nonprofit organizations. Service projects. Missionaries. Volunteers. Public servants. Heroes from all walks of life. And yet we are bombarded with feature stories of destruction and darkness, with an occasional sidebar of goodness.

With more and more people making kindness an instinctive part of life and instilling this value in the next generation, we can overpower the negative forces that steal the spotlight; we can force them into the background. We can make a case for kindness that is so loud it will be heard across the globe, reverberating long after our days on this great earth.

In addition to the hundreds of suggestions for showing kindness throughout these chapters, I am certain you have many ideas of your own to add to the mix. As our eyes are increasingly fixed on reaching out to others, we will see different opportunities within our own surroundings. Our experiences will be unique *and* unified. I realized very quickly, as I compiled the action steps for each kindness topic, that I could barely scratch the surface. There are simply too many ways to love one another! It's a great problem to have.

The good news is that the pure volume of ways to spread kindness makes committing to forty consecutive days of kindness more doable than we might anticipate. I was concerned when I first began my project that I would run out of ideas, but I could not have been more mistaken. There is no end to the possibilities.

A daily kindness practice (whether it is forty days or another timeline that better suits your life) is a perfect first step to making a case for kindness. Through our own actions, we will see firsthand the extraordinary difference we can make in ordinary moments. Creating a habit of kindness will ignite a fire in us that we can use to bring light and warmth to the world.

In Matthew 5:15–16, we are told: "No one lights a lamp and then puts it under a basket. Instead, a lamp is placed on a stand, where it gives light to everyone in the house. In the same way, let your good deeds shine out for all to see, so that everyone will praise your heavenly Father."

But how?

How do we let our light shine? How can we broaden the reach of our good deeds, even while we encourage everyone to recognize and praise our Father as they see His face in our goodness?

One way to accomplish this sacred mission is through a Kindness Initiative. Invite a group of people to join you in scattering seeds. Multiply the acts of kindness you produce by adding many hands, many hearts. Create unity through a profound, shared experience. You'll find more details for beginning a Kindness Initiative in the next section.

If we all lead a charge for kindness, looking to our daily lives for a group of people to join us, we can *each* be the catalyst for *thousands* of good deeds, *thousands* of seeds. Not to mention the changed hearts along the way (including our own) and the legacy we'll leave behind. Many people desire more opportunities to serve or to give, but they don't know where to begin. This is where to begin! We can show them. We can lead them.

Ah, kindness. It's something we can all agree on. Something we can do together to make a difference wherever we are; something that enables us to leave the world better than we found it. We have the light of Christ, and we are called to carry it with us throughout our ordinary days. I'm ready. Are you with me? Let's go and make a case for kindness!

Dear friends, since God loved us that much,
we surely ought to love each other. No one has ever seen God.
But if we love each other, God lives in us,
and his love is brought to full expression in us.

1 JOHN 4:11–12

CREATING A KINDNESS INITIATIVE WITH THE FIVE C'S

A Kindness Initiative is an informed invitation to spread kindness. It is the act of reaching out to a group of people, small or large, welcoming them into a forty-day kindness adventure, and providing the necessary resources to get started.

Why not multiply your acts of love and lead a Kindness Initiative within your community? The simple steps detailed in the Five C's will guide you through the process.

Community

Commitment

Cards

Compile

Communicate

COMMUNITY: Identify Your People

Think about the groups of people within your daily life that you could invite into a Kindness Initiative. Some possibilities are family, friends, church groups, coworkers, classrooms or schools, scout troops, sports teams, neighborhoods, book clubs, service groups, campus organizations, youth groups, and even online communities.

COMMITMENT: Make It Official

Establish a way for participants to sign up. This formality builds a sense of commitment and togetherness, and it motivates others to join in. A physical sign-up sheet in a central location is effective. I would recommend asking for email addresses, so you can reach out to participants if you wish. In addition, you could designate a few registration days for people to sign up for Forty Days of Kindness.

An online sign-up strategy is also a possibility, depending on the population—check out SignUpGenius.com. You might even consider creating a private Facebook group.

CARDS: Sneak Some Kindness; Leave a Card

Provide kindness cards or equip your participants to make kindness cards.

Creating kindness cards is an exciting step in preparing for a kindness project. The process of choosing the perfect words to represent your personal journey or your Kindness Initiative sparks the spirit of kindness! You will find a selection of quotes and verses in Appendix 3. You could also simply say: "Kindness is contagious . . . Pass it on."

Once you have selected your favorite inspirational words, there are three possible ways to create kindness cards: by hand, on your home computer, or through a professional printing service.

Anything handwritten these days is extra special. Adults and kids alike can create kindness cards the old fashioned way. You can use blank Avery printable business cards, or cut pieces of cardstock to the size of a business card. Then grab some markers and go to town. As you prepare for your Kindness Initiative, consider giving your participants a list of quotes and verses, along with blank cards. They can then choose their own quote and design kindness cards for their journey. Cards are not always needed for an act of kindness, so each participant will only need about ten cards for a forty-day kindness journey.

Depending on the size of your group, or if you are flying solo for Forty Days of Kindness, you may choose to print kindness cards from home. The Avery business cards mentioned above can help you accomplish this task. You can use their templates to create personalized and professional looking cards from your computer. When purchasing this product, note that there are different selections for ink jet versus laser printers. And if you would like cards that are printable on both sides, the products will have a specification for that as well.

Professional printing is another possibility for creating kindness cards. Any office store or online company that makes business cards will also make kindness cards. If you are doing Forty Days of Kindness with a large group, this is a great option. For our Kindness Initiative at church, we designed and printed kindness cards on VistaPrint.com. Perhaps a technologically savvy friend in your group would kindly create the cards. I have included a couple of samples in Appendix 2.

Kindness cards are fun to create and exhilarating to receive. Certain acts of kindness are gloriously amplified by having a card to leave behind. And if the recipient decides to "pass it on," we never know where our card might land.

I hope you enjoy this part of the process; meaningful kindness cards will set the stage for your adventure.

COMPILE: Create a "Kindness-To-Go" List

Help others get started by making a list of ideas to keep on hand for referencing and reflecting. There is a sample Kindness-To-Go List in Appendix 2. The items you choose to include in your list may vary depending on your group. Flip back through the pages of this book and pick out acts of kindness that work best—you could even pull one suggestion from each of the forty chapters. Then compile your list and distribute it to your participants. You'll notice that the sample list has sixty suggestions, but there is no magic number.

COMMUNICATE: Write It and Ignite It!

Encourage people to document their experience. Even if you aren't a big journaler, I would recommend giving this a try. Remembering our actions and processing our emotions and insights can tremendously enhance the kindness journey. If your brain is anything like mine, even the most exhilarating event or fascinating thought can be forgotten before the sun sets. Capturing kindness in writing keeps the experience alive and active. Infinitely!

One family who participated in Forty Days of Kindness made a kindness chart for each of their children (see Appendix 2). The kids documented their acts of kindness each day. These memories serve as a valued keepsake and a continual source of encouragement to keep on sprinkling kindness.

Another great way to ignite kindness is by sharing experiences and reactions with one another: create a Facebook page, a central notebook or sticky notes on a bulletin board, a designated email address, a mural, a website, a photo collage, or a celebration at the end of the forty days where people can share their experiences face to face. A participating church wrapped up their journey with a segment in the church bulletin. The Forty Days of Kindness Committee thanked participants and lifted up some of the acts of kindness shown throughout their community.

Five simple steps can lead to limitless reach as we link arms with others to create an eruption of kindness.

A bright blue sign at the edge of my church's parking lot sums up our call to serve, our responsibility to make a difference. It declares, "You are now entering the mission field." It isn't enough to know what to do, the more critical step is doing it. That is where we are today, as we near the exit of these pages. We have the inspiration and the information to embrace a life of kindness. Now we can put it into action. I can't wait to see you on the mission field! Together we will brighten up the world, one act of love at time.

SAMPLE SELECTIONS FOR GETTING STARTED

When you create your kindness cards, Appendix 3 will serve as a great resource for finding the perfect quote or verse for the Forty days of Kindness. The following are card models for various audiences.

Kindness Card for General Audiences

I expect to pass through life but once.
If therefore, there be any kindness
I can show, or any good thing I can do
to any fellow being, let me do it now,
and not defer or neglect it,
as I shall not pass this way again.

William Penn

(Front)

Kindness is Contagious...

Pass it on.

(Back)

Kindness Card for Church

We love because God first loved us.
1 John 4:19

God's work. Our hands.

(Front)

Kindness is Contagious...

Pass it on.

(Back)

Kindness Card for Kids

Love changes everything.
So fill the world with it.

Anonymous

(Front)

Kind is the new cool.

Pay it forward.

(Back)

Sample Kids' Kindness Chronicle

Kids will enjoy keeping track of their daily acts of kindness. These charts are particularly useful for younger children who might not be able to write full journal entries. For older kids and adults, journaling is recommended, but if you prefer this method . . . go for it.

When you recreate this document, you can make it two-sided and get all forty days on one sheet. Consider making these available for your Kindness Initiative.

Date	Forty Days of Kindness: Kids Daily Kindness Chronicle
11/1	Did the dishes without being asked.
11/2	Offered my snack to a friend.
11/3	Picked up trash that wasn't mine.
11/4	Community service project with my family.
11/5	Gave a classmate some chocolate and a note.
11/6	Asked someone to play with me and my friend at recess.
11/7	Let someone go in front of me in line at lunch.
11/8	Gave up my really good seat on the bus.
11/9	Did a chore when it wasn't my turn.
11/10	Helped someone even though they aren't always nice to me.
11/11	Took a muffin to my teacher.
11/12	Donated two dollars of my own money to charity.
11/13	Made my sister's bed.
11/14	Donated books I've outgrown to the nursery at church.

Sample Kindness-To-Go List

Create a double-sided handout for your Kindness Initiative, or for your own use during Forty Days of Kindness. You can adapt these suggestions to reflect your own ideas and other acts of kindness shared in this book.

1. Write a letter of appreciation to someone who impacted your life.
2. Make dinner for a friend.
3. Take a bottle of water to someone working outside on a hot day (or hot chocolate on a cold day).
4. Tape a sandwich bag of coins to a vending machine or parking meter.
5. Leave an umbrella at a bus stop on a rainy day.
6. Give blood.
7. Take in your neighbor's trashcans after trash pick up.
8. Visit someone who is homebound.
9. Leave an inspirational book, magazine, or a fun toy in a waiting room.
10. Slip a gift card into a random book at a book store.
11. Bake cookies for your mail carrier.
12. Set a few stamps on the prep table at the post office.
13. Send a package or letter to a friend or family member just because.
14. Let someone go in front of you in line.
15. Surprise a stranger by paying off their lay-a-way.
16. Give up that great parking spot.
17. Write positive messages in sidewalk chalk at a playground.

18. Put together a writing kit with stationary, envelopes, stamps and a pen, and leave it at a hospital or nursing home.
19. Drop off a teddy bear to a police station or fire department for the kids they serve.
20. Pay the toll for the person behind you.
21. Treat the car behind you at a drive-thru window.
22. Leave a basket of outside toys at a local park for the kids to find and enjoy.
23. Make a struggling family's summer by buying them a season pass to a pool.
24. Bring food to the food bank.
25. Donate your old cell phones to the National Coalition against Domestic Violence (ncadv.org).
26. Let the management know when someone did a great job.
27. Forgive someone. Repeat as necessary.
28. Buy a book for a child at booksforkids.org.
29. Send a funny YouTube video to a friend having a tough day.
30. Do something sweet for your spouse—breakfast in bed, wash his/her car, make a favorite dinner or dessert.
31. Reach out to someone who is standing alone at a party.
32. Be patient while driving.
33. Leave a few dollars in an aisle at the dollar store with a note.
34. You know that game you really don't enjoy playing with your kids but they love it? Do that—for a long time.
35. Plant flowers in a neglected area.
36. Bring supplies to a local pet shelter.
37. Hold a friend's baby so he or she can enjoy having free hands.
38. Send flowers to your parents.

39. Bring a treat to a residence hall for college students to enjoy.

40. Make a donation to an organization that is meaningful to you or your family.

41. Triple the tip.

42. Anonymously pay for the meal of someone at a restaurant.

43. Spend time with a friend you haven't seen in a while.

44. Say yes at the store when asked to donate a dollar to charity.

45. Make a bird feeder.

46. Create kindness bookmarks with your kids and slip them into books at the library.

47. Bring fresh produce to a new neighbor.

48. Leave sticky notes in random places with words of encouragement.

49. Offer to take a friend's carpool shift.

50. Bring a special snack to share with your coworkers.

51. Send a package or letter to someone in the military.

52. Ask to pay for another person's items at the dry cleaner. (Consider doing this for a public servant like a police officer.)

53. Leave some coupons at the grocery store.

54. Bring popsicles to a busy park on a hot day.

55. Encourage your kids to start a piggy bank for a cause.

56. Smile at 5 strangers today!

57. Call a local homeless shelter and ask how you can help.

58. Give a stranger a sincere compliment.

59. Drive someone to a doctor appointment.

60. Be a mentor.

FUEL FOR FORTY DAYS: VERSES AND QUOTES

Bible verses and quotes are energizing—certain to jazz up a Forty Days of Kindness project.

One participant, Joyce, filled a shallow, wallet-sized box with forty cards. On each card, she wrote a kindness quote for each day and gave the box to her grandchildren. Every day at dinner, they would read the quote and talk about their act of kindness for that day. If you choose to replicate this idea, you could also use recipe cards and a recipe box, or notecards and a notecard box. Quote cards can serve as an alternative to journaling if you write your act of kindness on the back of the card each day.

Quotes and verses can be used in a daily e-mail or Facebook post during your journey, on kindness cards, or they can be printed out and attached to a bulletin board. A quote for the day could also be shared on a chalkboard or dry-erase board at home, work, or school. If you choose to incorporate inspirational words as part of your outreach, the following pages are a selection of my favorites and some fun options for kids.

Do all the good you can, by all the means you can, in all the ways you can, in all the places you can, at all the times you can, to all the people you can, as long as ever you can.

—John Wesley

Kindness is like snow; it beautifies everything it covers.

—Anonymous

As small as it may seem, a good deed is always worth the doing.

—Spark Matsunaga

I am only one, but I am still one. I cannot do everything, but still I can do something. And because I cannot do everything, I will not refuse to do the something that I can do.

—Helen Keller

Be kind, for everyone you meet is fighting a hard battle.

—Plato

Kind words can be short and easy to speak, but their echoes are truly endless.

—Mother Theresa

Kindness is the evidence of greatness.

—Charles Fenno Hoffman

Do to others as you would like them to do to you.

—Luke 6:31

Don't think too much about yourself. Try to cultivate the habit of thinking of others; this will reward you.

—Charles W. Eliot

Kindness is a hard thing to give away. It keeps coming back to the giver.

—Ralph Scott

I expect to pass through life but once. If therefore, there be any kindness I can show, or any good thing I can do to any fellow being, let me do it now, and not defer or neglect it, as I shall not pass this way again.

—William Penn

Your own soul is nourished when you are kind; it is destroyed when you are cruel.

—Proverbs 11:17 TLB

Kind words are the music of the world.

—Frederick William Faber

Those who bring sunshine into the lives of others cannot keep it from themselves.

—James M. Barrie

The first question which the priest and the Levite asked was: "If I stop to help this man, what will happen to me?" But . . . the Good Samaritan reversed the question: "If I do not stop to help this man, what will happen to him?"

—Martin Luther King Jr.

Let us learn to live with kindness, to love everyone, even when they do not love us.

—Pope Francis

No one has ever seen God; but if we love one another, God lives in us and his love is made complete in us.

—1 John 4:12 NIV

I still believe, in spite of everything, that people are truly good at heart.

—Anne Frank

Anxiety weighs down the heart, but a kind word cheers it up.

—Proverbs 12:25 NIV

Be kind to one another, tenderhearted, forgiving one another as God in Christ forgave you.

—Ephesians 4:32 NKJV

Since you get more joy out of giving to others, you should put a good deal of thought into the happiness that you are able to give.

—Eleanor Roosevelt

What does love look like? It has the hands to help others. It has the feet to hasten to the poor and needy. It has eyes to see misery and want. It has the ears to hear the sighs and sorrows of men. That is what love looks like.

—St. Augustine

Carry out a random act of kindness, with no expectation of reward, safe in the knowledge that one day someone might do the same for you.

—Princess Diana

Think of ways to motivate one another to acts of love and good works.

—Hebrews 10:24

Do not let kindness and truth leave you; bind them around your neck, write them on the tablet of your heart.

—Proverbs 3:3 NASB

Be devoted to one another in love. Honor one another above yourselves.

—Romans 12:10 NIV

Serve God by doing common actions in a heavenly spirit, and then, if your daily calling only leaves you cracks and crevices of time, fill them up with holy service.

—Charles Spurgeon

Command them to do good, to be rich in good deeds, and to be generous and willing to share.

—1 Timothy 6:18 NIV

A tree is known by its fruit; a man by his deeds. A good deed is never lost; he who sows courtesy reaps friendship, and he who plants kindness gathers love.

—Saint Basil

Kids' Corner

Be somebody who makes everybody feel like a somebody.
—Anonymous

A little consideration, a little thought for others, makes all the difference.
—A. A. Milne, *Winnie the Pooh*

Unless someone like you cares a whole awful lot, nothing is going to get better. It's not.
—Dr. Seuss, *The Lorax*

No act of kindness, no matter how small, is ever wasted.
—Aesop

Somewhere inside all of us is the power to change the world.
—Roald Dahl

You have been my friend," replied Charlotte, "that in itself is a tremendous thing."
—E. B. White, *Charlotte's Web*

So encourage each other and build each other up.
1 Thessalonians 5:11

We love because [God] first loved us.
—1 John 4:19 NIV

APPENDIX 4

CHARITABLE ORGANIZATIONS

The following is a list of the websites for charitable organizations and agencies mentioned throughout this book. Of course, don't forget about your local churches. Please feel free to research and find other organizations you find worth giving to or helping through.

unitedway.org

volunteermatch.org

createthegood.org

serve.gov

pointsoflight.org

greatnonprofits.org

guidestar.org

SAtruck.org

purpleheartpickup.org

LionsClub.org

GlassSlipperProject.org

NCADV.org

heifer.org

worldvision.org

convoyofhope.org

IJM.org

watertothrive.org

LocksOfLove.org

redcross.org

RedCrossBlood.org

BeTheMatch.org

OrganDonor.gov

friendsassoc.org

211.org

endhomelessness.org

nationalhomelessness.org

standupforkids.org

UniteforHer.org

medgift.com

caringbridge.org

100womenwhocarecc.org

alexslemonade.org

ColoraSmile.org

AmericanBible.org

ReachOutAndRead.org

NationalLiteracyDirectory.org

OperationPaperback.org

LittleFreeLibrary.org

MealTrain.com

TakeThemAMeal.com

ACKNOWLEDGEMENTS

To my husband Josh: You have been my copilot through this adventure from the very first moment. You know, the one where you held my kindness journal in your hand and said, "This would make a great book." And so it began. Thank you for your unwavering love and support. Life is simply better with you by my side.

To my three kids, my partners in kindness, Ellie, Jack, and Charlie: This project has been a team effort, and nothing was more motivating than your enthusiasm and encouragement. Getting to be your mom is my absolute favorite thing.

To my parents, Joe and Tina Ray: For selflessly supporting me always, even when my plans may have seemed unreasonable. You made me believe I could do anything.

To my brother Mark: My biggest cheerleader. My comic relief.

To Julie Freund Wall: For your constant reassurance to keep moving forward, and for saying yes each time I asked you for a giant, time-consuming favor. The gifts of your wisdom, time, and devoted friendship mean the world to me.

To Amber Marcoon: Who would have thought a lunch date and a road trip to She Speaks would have led us here? Thank you for using your incredible talents to help me along every step of this journey. I cherish your friendship and your continual prayers.

To my publisher, Pamela Clements: The pages of this book are covered with your gentle guidance, patience, and grace—but most of all, your kindness. Thank you for the opportunity to share this message. I am sincerely grateful for you and the awesome team at Worthy Inspired.

To my church family at Calvary Lutheran Church: For being a part of this experience as the very first Kindness Initiative! It is an honor to join hands with all of you as we give glory to God and share Christ's love.

To countless friends and family members who lifted me up throughout this process: Thank you, thank you so much. I love you all.

To everyone who allowed me to share their beautiful stories: This book would not have been possible without you. May your kindness continue to ripple.

ABOUT THE AUTHOR

LISA BARRICKMAN is a Licensed Professional Counselor, community volunteer, and first-time author. She has a BS in Psychology from the University of Dayton and an MA in Pastoral Counseling from Loyola University in Maryland.

Her early career days were joyfully spent in student affairs at the university level. After receiving her counseling license, she worked for many years as a therapist in a Christian counseling practice, then continued to use her counseling skills daily as a stay-at-home mom!

She and her husband, Josh, grew up in Ashtabula, Ohio, and they live in West Chester, Pennsylvania, with three busy kids and a tireless Boston Terrier named Yoda.

A 2015 recipient of The President's Volunteer Service Award, Lisa has a heart for Jesus and wants her life to reflect His love.

She loves walking, reading, and watching any field, court, or stage that her children are on—preferably with a big mug of coffee in hand.

You can connect with Lisa on her blog at
www.LisaBarrickman.com

**IF YOU ENJOYED THIS BOOK, WILL YOU CONSIDER
SHARING THE MESSAGE WITH OTHERS?**

Mention the book in a blog post or through Facebook, Twitter, Pinterest, or upload a picture through Instagram.

Recommend this book to those in your small group, book club, workplace, and classes.

Head over to facebook.com/worthypublishing, "LIKE" the page, and post a comment as to what you enjoyed the most.

Tweet "I recommend reading #ACaseForKindness by Lisa Barrickman @worthypub"

Pick up a copy for someone you know who would be challenged and encouraged by this message.

Write a book review online.

Visit us at worthypublishing.com

 twitter.com/worthypub

 worthypub.tumblr.com

 facebook.com/worthypublishing

 pinterest.com/worthypub

 instagram.com/worthypub

 youtube.com/worthypublishing